Presented to:

_____

From:

_____

Date:

_____

What My Cat Has Taught Me About Life

Meditations for Cat Lovers

by
Niki Anderson

Honor Books

Tulsa, Oklahoma

2nd Printing

What My Cat Has Taught Me About Life
— Meditations for Cat Lovers
ISBN 1-56292-466-4
Copyright © 1997 by Niki Anderson
P. O. Box 30222
Spokane, WA 99223-3003

Published by Honor Books, Inc.
P. O. Box 55388
Tulsa, Oklahoma 74155

Dedication

Dedicated to my mother,

who inspired both my affection for cats and my passion for God;

to my husband for his enduring and patient support;

to my daughter for her journalistic ear;

and to my son for his daily pats on the shoulder.

Acknowledgments

Thanks to my editor, Cristine Bolley, for her idea of a cat lover's meditation book;

to all the willing folks who shared their cat stories;

to my brother, Michael, for believing in me;

to Dr. Kevin A. French, D.V.M., for his careful review of the cat tips;

to my friends who encouraged my seclusion to write this book;

to writer and friend, Betty Egbert, for her keen edit;

and to all those who granted permission for borrowed material.

Contents

Introduction 11

Embrace Courage 12

Trust Your Heart 16

Credible People Recognize Im-paws-tors 20

Discretion — A Wise Cousin to Prudence 24

Postures Nurture Confidence 27

Balance Is Somewhere In Between 30

A Good Attitude Brings Good Fortune 34

Sacrificial Sharing Makes Best Friends 38

The Cost of Peacemaking 42

Be Finicky About Your Choice of Words 46

Everyone Supervises Someone 50

Faith Surmounts the Highest Peaks .54

Secrets Are for Keeps 58

Dreams Can Come True 62

Tenacity — The Grit of Conviction .65

Affirm Someone Every Day 68

The Great Tutor of Experience 72

Never Stamp Out Hope 76

Perseverance — The Push of Pursuit 79

Love Eases the Stress of Patience 82

Opportunity Waits for the Watchful .86

Beware of Jealousy 89

Forgiveness Brings Warmth 92

The Joy of Generosity 96

Everybody Deserves To Be Rescued 100

Anger Isn't Always Bad 104

Devotion Is More Than a Prayer 107

Boundaries Signal Privacy 110

There's a Good Side of Change 114

Counsel Focuses Vision 118

Decorum — More Than Manners 122

Determination Launches Initiative 125

Make Your World a Playground 128

Everyone Benefits From Community 132

Widen Your Horizons 136

Polite Confrontation Averts Angry Disputes 140

The Two-Way Toggle of Friendship 144

Happiness Is an Outlook 148

Share the Sunshine 151

The Soft Sound of Humility 154

Individuality Is Your Imprint 158

A Powerful Force Called Influence 162

Let Your Limits Expand You 165

Moderation Pays Great Rewards 168

Value Is Not Based on Purr-chase Price 172

Always Make a Clean Impression .176

Keep an Overhead Perspective 180

Introduction

This book is for cat lovers — those charmed by the cat's inscrutable ways, calmed by their purring, awed by their grace, and fascinated by their personalities — those who will always find delight in the cat.

Each story spotlights characteristics of domestic cats and will cause readers to smile and recall, "Oh yes, I've seen cats do that." The stories may bring a tear to your eye or make you laugh, as a cat's touching ways lift your heart or their antics tickle you.

Also included are tips for proper care of your cats. Veterinarian-approved information and recommendations will teach you about topics as varied as identification microchips and fur balls.

And, the meditations serve in another way. Each anecdote springboards a principle which gives you a wise view of life from a cat's purr-spective. The themes center on the everyday issues of life and present strategies for coping. For example, in "Polite Confrontation Averts Angry Disputes," the cat's advice about responding to anger is, "Twitch your tail gently to express your annoyance, lest you resort to scratching!"

In the midst of the crushing pressures we face today, believe it or not, cats can help! I have found that feline philosophy is sometimes akin to divine instruction. God has often taught me through my cats. Again and again I gain insight through the actions of my furry pals.

So I invite you to sit back, relax, and enjoy ins-purr-ation for daily living from the world of cats!

Embrace Courage

*"Attempting great feats
calls for courage."*

Dennis

"Dennis, be quiet!" shouted my husband. Dennis was a mischievous six-month-old kitten whose antics frequently rallied our family of four. He could get our entire household in an uproar within minutes. Late one afternoon, Dennis did just that when he disappeared.

12

Every family member scoured the house from attic to basement, but to no avail. We moved the search outdoors, and our united hunt soon ended when we heard a mournful wail atop a stately pine tree in our neighbor's backyard. At the welcome sight of his rescuers, Dennis revealed his sense of relief with a faint mew.

Bob assessed various rescue options and made a quick on-site decision. I then watched in amazement as my husband hugged the tread of the trunk and began scaling upward twenty-five feet.

"Careful Dad!" The kids viewed their Dad's risk-taking as an unmistakable sign of devotion. "Dad must *really* like Dennis," one said in awe.

As for me, I simply held my breath. The stranded cat situation was not as cat-astrophic to me as seeing my husband, glove-less and ladder-less, forge skyward. Soon I was beholding not one, but *two* of my loved ones high in the proud pine. Minutes later, and to my great relief, Bob descended clutching the recovered kitten. The family headed home with our furry trophy in arms.

Cat Nip:

Fraid E. Cat never caught a mouse.

13

Paws for Prayer:

Dear God, remind me to pray rather than fear when I am confronted with danger. Amen.

"Fear not, for I am with you; be not dismayed, for I am your God. I will strengthen you, yes, I will help you."
Isaiah 41:10 NKJV[1]

Though cats often make brave ascents, their descent is sometimes paralyzed by fear. They have plenty of courage for the easy part, but freeze when they look down on the difficulty of maneuvering a descent.

Since that day, I have noticed that fear shunts both the start and finish of many feats. I have seen the fear of rejection hinder an offer of help, the fear of criticism silence a possible solution, and the fear of obstacles preclude the birth of an organization. Danger lurks in every endeavor, but I am learning not to pussyfoot around with fear. If I get into trouble, like Dennis, I mew loudly and try to remember that God will never leave me stranded on a limb.

Cat Tip:

If your cat is vigorously and frequently scratching the ears, a yeast infection or ear mites may be the irritant. Medication is necessary. Visit your veterinarian.

The Tail End:

Danger feared is folly; danger faced is freedom.
— *Dr. V. Raymond Edman*

Trust Your Heart

"Never doubt your way. Instinct will direct at important junctures."

16

When Sam's family, the Thompsons, moved from Wisconsin to Arizona in 1986, they took Sam with them. A year later, financial stresses forced them to return to Wisconsin. The Thompsons left Sam behind at Tucson Humane Society, optimistic that he would be adopted. Sam had only one thought at the animal shelter. "Let meow 'ta here!"

For days Sam studied every movement around him, looking for a way out so he could get back to his family. Then one day an opportunity to depart presented itself, and Sam escaped.

Only God knows the trials, terrors, and difficulties Sam encountered in the journey that followed. Yet this Siamese cat never gave up and never lost hope of seeing his family again. His only guides were instinct and devotion, but they proved quite enough.

One day — 1,429 miles and four years later — Sam suddenly appeared on the back doorstep of the Wisconsin house where he and the Thompsons had lived. Luckily, the new homeowners recognized Sam. They immediately called Mrs. Thompson to tell her that Sam had come home.

When Mrs. Thompson arrived, Sam *leapt* into her arms. Though thinner and older, he had reached his destination.[2]

17

Cat Nip:

A cat will come to "kitty, kitty, kitty," if not engaged in anything more interesting.

Paws for Prayer:

Dear Lord, help me choose every right path, avenue, and highway necessary to arrive at my goals. Amen.

"You are the God who performs miracles."
Psalm 77:14

Reaching goals is sometimes a long and mapless journey. Setting out is like a walk in the dark. Only by keeping the destination close at heart, will travelers find the determination to bypass distractions and the strength to endure roadside troubles. The journey toward achievement is not for the diffident! Sam reached his destination for three reasons: he followed his heart, he trusted his instincts, and he kept traveling.

Cat Tip:

To assist owners in locating a lost cat, many choose to have the kitty tattooed on the inner flank with a serial number and listed in one of the national registries. A veterinarian administers mild sedation and performs the quick and harmless procedure. An implanted microchip is more frequently recommended.

The Tail End:

Even if you're on the right track, you'll get run over if you just sit there.

— *Will Rogers*

Credible People Recognize Im-paws-tors

"Never believe a purple cat."

Purple Cat

20

Carol bred Manx, Siamese, and Scottish Folds for thirty-three years and boarded all varieties of cats, including some of ours, for over a decade. She had seen hundreds of color variations among the majority of existing cat breeds.

One afternoon, she received a telephone call. The caller began, "Hello, my veterinarian told me you could duplicate my cat if *anyone* could. I want another cat just like the one I recently bought. She's purple."

Carol corrected her slightly and replied, "Oh, you mean a Siamese Lilacpointe. Yes, I can find you one."

"No, you don't understand. She isn't Siamese, and she has long-hair."

"But there is no truly purple cat."

"Well, if you don't believe me, I'll bring her over." The caller's tone reflected her offense over Carol's dubious reaction. Carol invited her to come. She watched at her gate as the woman plucked a purple pussycat from her car. In a glance, Carol identified the breed as a Cymric Manx, and concluded that the previous owner had color dyed the vivid fur.

Carol showed the woman the places on the wrists and mouth where the cat had licked the dye off her skin, but still the new owner insisted the cat was a unique species. She left in a huff.

Cat Nip:

A cat's affection is sought after more than a cat's markings, sex, size, or breed.

21

Paws for Prayer:

Dear God, as I work to rid my life of my own inward deceit, make me patient with the incredulous traits of others. Amen.

"For the LORD does not see as man sees; for man looks at the outward appearance, but the LORD looks at the heart."
1 Samuel 16:7 NKJV

Carol's knowledge and experience as a breeder, boarder, and show judge made her "cat credible." Credible people are true from the inside out. But non-credible people are shades of one color on the inside, while wearing colors that deceive on the outside. Authentic people are credible, and it is they, not purple cats, who are the truly special breed.

Cat Tip:

Persians (and other cats) are vulnerable to highly contagious ringworm, a fungal disease, located most often on the cat's ears, face, neck, and tail. The hair breaks off or falls out, causing a round bald spot with scaly skin in the center and an advancing red edge. Disinfection and antibiotics over a long period of time are required for healing.

The Tail End:

*Credibility is the warp and woof
in the garment of character.*

Discretion — A Wise Cousin to Prudence

"Learn to leave before someone says 'scat.'"

Krazy Kat

According to a word-of-mouth account passed among several neighbors, Krazy Kat was the sole survivor of a litter of kittens suspected of being cruelly beaten in a riddance effort. The neighbor who found and pitied the crying kitten delivered the little survivor to Mrs. Rasmussen, who was known for adopting stray animals.

The kitten recovered, although her growth was stunted. Her legs were so short they were barely visible. She acted in unconventional ways most of her life — like jumping in the middle of people's backs, herding the goats with the farm collie, and joining Mr. Rasmussen on his rabbit hunts in the back field.

Much to the annoyance of the Rasmussen's black banty hen, Krazy stalked the chicken continuously. One afternoon, the banty was weary with brooding over her six chicks and lost patience with Krazy's unrelenting interest. With no more warning than a few angry clucks, she flew into Krazy with the fury of a protective mother. Orange fur flew.

Humiliated and defeated, Krazy slinked along the ground, seeking refuge from the incensed hen. From that day forward, discretion was Krazy's new name. Before venturing outdoors, she always paused at the door to make sure the banty was nowhere close by. In all her goings, she cut a wide path around the capricious hen. Krazy read the caution signs and knew when to scat.

🐾 Cat Nip:

What is the female cat's favorite department store for purrse and purrl purrchases? Cats Fifth Avenue.[3]

Paws for Prayer:

Dear God, help me know when the wisest move is to simply vanish. Amen.

"Discretion will protect you, and understanding will guard you."
Proverbs 2:11

Cats are intuitively wise about making themselves scarce. If there's a lot of commotion, cats scat. Dogs start barking when things get tense, but cats simply leave. A carefully timed departure is just as important as a carefully timed entrance. When relationships heat up, departing is sometimes the most discreet action to take.

Cat Tip:

Most kittens adjust to a comfortable collar without showing signs of annoyance. Collars that stretch allow the kitten to wiggle out of the collar if it became noosed and would otherwise strangle. If you plan to walk your cat on a leash, a chest harness is preferred to a collar. Begin when the cats are kittens.

The Tail End:

It is better to be pleasantly absent, than to be miserably present.

Postures Nurture Confidence

*"When you're frightened, arch your back
and believe you're a lot bigger."*

*P*epper's body language signaled the presence of a canine intruder, common at the Breckenridge farm. Mottled black and white Pepper often patrolled the wildflower border between the county road and the farm property. Big dogs, stray dogs, visiting dogs, and lost dogs passed by daily. Though each odoriferous wanderer was usually many times Pepper's size, she was not intimidated — at least not judging by her body language.

One afternoon as Mr. Breckenridge strolled to the mailbox, he noticed Pepper on guard duty. Along came sprightly Mr. Giant Dog who spotted Pepper and advanced with light steps and a harmless persona. But his malevolent intent did not escape Pepper. She read his thoughts — "Bite cat, or better yet, eat cat." Mr. Breckenridge saw the apprehension in Pepper's squinted eyes.

Pepper's arched back, bushed out fur, flattened ears, and stiff legs caused Mr. Giant Dog to hesitate. He made a sliding stop, cocked his head, and reconsidered. Pepper didn't relax her fortress-like posture. Mr. Giant Dog then made a U-turn and tripped back to the main road to search for less menacing entertainment.

Cat Nip:

It is an enigma why millions of cat owners tolerate feline hauteur.

Paws for Prayer:

Dear God, make my body language always convey expressions of my confidence in You. Amen.

"So do not throw away your confidence; it will be richly rewarded."
Hebrews 10:35

Pepper's confident posture emboldened her and disarmed the dog. Postures of the body often give courage to the soul. Smiling dissipates fear, raising the chin diminishes inferiority, and a positive answer emboldens a trembling heart. The words we say ("I know I can if I try."), the attitude we embrace ("It may be difficult, but it's possible."), and the action we take ("Let's give it all we've got.") are postures of confidence that give God a chance to show what He can do.

Cat Tip:

Dogs and cats accept one another best when they are acquired together as kittens and puppies. Bring home two kittens from the same litter, or a puppy and kitten at the same time, which allows the two to grow up together and learn early to enjoy and love each other.

The Tail End:

The most diffident can become the most confident, through faith in God.

Balance Is Somewhere In Between

*"Balance your victuals between
a little and a lot."*

"Tom Cat"

When my brother and his wife moved from the city to the country, they soon learned their residence was shared with twenty-two emaciated barn cats. The table scraps Mike offered the shabby bunch were obviously the cats' first and only diet

30

supplement. Mice had been their staple. Mike tossed the scraps about twenty-five feet from the house since the wild cats would venture no closer. Each night the hungry lot emerged from the shadows, slinked forward, and scarfed all the edibles.

Among the skinny felines was one sizable tomcat who was bolder than the rest. Over time, he and Mike developed a relationship through Mike's generosity. When a friend who bagged an elk that season gave Mike thirty pounds of the scraps, Mike scattered the red meat and white fat for his feline boarders. The tidbits proved irresistible to the skittish cats.

Thanksgiving Day arrived and the cats also arrived to await a share in the largess of the holiday. By then the big tomcat's penchant for scraps had surpassed his phobia of people. He would snatch morsels right from Mike's hand. In the spirit of the holiday, Mike offered him seconds, thirds, fifths, and tenths. He finally quit counting. The tom cat was satiated at last and withdrew, too full to partake further. Perhaps for the first time in an encounter with food, he refused.

 Cat Nip:

Real men cuddle their cats.

31

Paws for Prayer:

Dear God, help me achieve balance by living free of both maximums and minimums. Amen.

"Give me neither poverty nor riches. Feed me with the food allotted to me."

Proverbs 30:8 NKJV

The abundance of Thanksgiving was an extreme contrast to the meager provisions on which the tomcat had long survived. That day he experienced the contrast between bounty and deficiency. Interestingly, both extremes brought discomfort — the bloat of gluttony or the pangs of hunger. Perhaps the tomcat returned to tell the other cats, "Enough is enough. Whether it be a few mice or a feast of turkey, I've learned that the best portion is a balance somewhere in between."

Cat Tip:

When grooming itself, a cat swallows hair which remains in the stomach and intestines. This causes the cat to vomit. To facilitate passage of hairballs, add a teaspoon of mineral oil to the cat's food for three consecutive days. One to two teaspoons of milk of magnesia on the fourth day may hasten the process.

The Tail End:

Balanced living occurs when the demands and provisions of life are counterpoised.

A Good Attitude Brings Good Fortune

"Keep a right cat-titude."

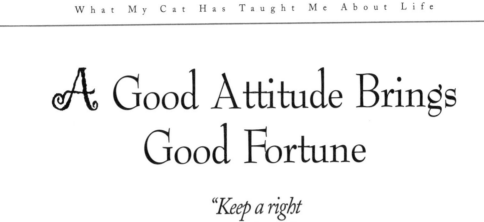

Gary

34

Male cats are not normally endowed with mothering instincts, neither are they happy for long in a Humane Society cell. But Gary, a large orange and white tabby, made the most of his temporary confinement at the local animal shelter. He turned his incarceration into an opportunity to nurture homeless kittens.

Soon after Gary was donated to the shelter, the staff named him "the baby-sitter." In his cell were a variety of breeds, sizes, and colors of cats and kittens. Several of the orphaned kittens tried unsuccessfully to entreat surrogate mothers, but the unwilling females refused their entreaties with loud spits and rude swats. Gary noticed.

One afternoon my husband and I visited the Humane Society to adopt a new cat. We requested a "nice male." The worker led us to Gary, who was propped in a corner with five kittens cuddled snugly against his white belly. The kittens blinked contentedly through slitted eyes. Gary appeared as gratified as a doting mother. "But," my husband corrected, "we want a *male*."

The staffer smiled. "You said you wanted a *nice* male? Sir, that cat's the nicest male you'll ever find. We call him the baby-sitter because he cares for those kittens like a responsible nanny. Periodically, he stands up and stretches and then relaxes again with 'his litter.' After he arrived all the kittens stopped crying."

35

Cat Nip:

Seen in a newspaper ad: "Free kittens: Mother — Snowy Persian; Father — From a nice neighborhood!"

Paws for Prayer:

Dear Lord, when I need an attitude change, help me discover the opportunities in my misfortunes. Amen.

"And we know that in all things God works for the good of those who love him."

Romans 8:28

When unpredicted confinements suddenly restrict life, the attitude we assume can redeem or condemn us. Gary looked around him and chose to find meaning in his predicament. His positive attitude helped him focus where he was and challenged him to meet an obvious need. Gary's good attitude also won him a new home. Bob and I adopted Gary the kitten-sitter that very day.

Cat Tip:

Neutering will cause male cats to become more placid since they are not driven to seek sexual partners. Their desire to fight diminishes and they become content with a smaller territory.

The Tail End:

We who lived in the concentration camps can remember the men who walked through the huts comforting others, giving away their last piece of bread. They may have been few in number, but they offer sufficient proof that everything can be taken from a man but one thing: The last of his freedoms—to choose one's attitude in any given set of circumstances.

— Viktor E. Frankl

Sacrificial Sharing Makes Best Friends

"Sacrificing may give someone a second life."

"His kidneys are failing," a Virginia veterinarian told the tearful owner of Smokey, an ailing gray and white cat. Sandy Carr and her husband, a childless couple, enjoyed a special love for Smokey, who was a stray the Carrs had found and adopted.

Reaching for hope, Sandy asked the vet if there was any possibility of a kidney transplant. The reluctant vet answered, "We could look into it, I suppose." The Carrs surfed the Internet that night and located several specialists who performed the operation. They chose the nearest clinic, which was 450 miles away in Buffalo.

The Buffalo veterinarian consented to begin a search for a kidney match, under the condition that the donor cat be selected from the Buffalo Society for the Prevention of Cruelty to Animals (S.P.C.A.) shelter. Two-thirds of the cats there were put to sleep because no one adopted them. He also insisted on a second condition. "After the transplant, you have to adopt the donor cat." The vet's kindhearted requirement would save two lives — the cat that would otherwise be euthanized and the cat that would otherwise die of kidney failure. Sandy was ecstatic. She gladly agreed to adopt the little "sustainer of life."

Both cats survived the four-and-a-half hour surgery. A kidney slightly smaller than a plum was removed from a buff-colored kitten donor and transplanted into Smokey. Two days later, Buffalo, the newly named kitten, went to his new home at the Carrs. Three weeks later, Smokey was ready to return home

39

Cat Nip:

Who is the cat's favorite actor and playwright? William Shakespurr[5]

and to meet Buffalo, the best friend of his life. Today the two cats are great buddies and will surely be friends fur-ever.[4]

Sharing doesn't always involve life-or-death consequences, but learning to share things of trivial importance increases the likelihood that we will find courage to share things of critical importance and even make sacrifices when necessary. Whenever we do, we usually make a friend fur life.

Cat Tip:

The skin condition usually generalized as "mange" is any of several chronic skin diseases in cats caused by parasitic mites and characterized by skin lesions (blisters sometimes), itching, loss of hair (bald areas), or severe dandruff. Mange caused by mites is highly contagious to other animals. Fur mite mange is contagious to humans but can be treated successfully with a selenium sulfide shampoo once weekly for three weeks.

Paws for Prayer:

Dear God, help me to be detached from things which have no lasting importance and willing to give sacrificially when I am faced with the challenge. Amen.

"And do not forget to do good and to share with others, for with such sacrifices God is pleased."
Hebrews 13:16

The Tail End:

Giving should be based on principle, regulated by system, (and) beautified by self-sacrifice.
— *The Cream Book*, compiled
by Keith L. Brooks

The Cost of Peacemaking

*"Being a peacemaker may
cause some fur to fly."*

Scooter

Ginger, my childhood red Shepherd, and our white cat Scooter were true comrades. When Ginger snoozed near the fireplace, Scooter snuggled against Ginger's pudgy tummy. In their mock fights, Scooter let Ginger hold his head in her jaws.

42

If an intruding cat or a hostile dog ventured onto the cat's territory, Ginger made quick pursuit in Scooter's defense. I was twelve years old when I witnessed an amazing rescue, as *Scooter saved Ginger* from an irascible dog.

It was long before the days of leash laws. I sat on the front porch stroking Ginger's head, when a Rottweiler strutted down the street. He darted from the curb to the porch in a flash. His sudden approach and the aggression in his eyes terrorized me, and Ginger was totally unprepared for the unprovoked attack which followed. "Stop! Get outta here!" I screamed. Helpless, I watched a blur of wrestling movements so rapid I couldn't distinguish one dog from another.

Scooter ambled around the corner of the garage just in time to see Ginger in grave trouble. To my astonishment, in a split second Scooter leaped into the middle of the fray. Now added to the snaps and growls were hisses and yowls and a tumbling white streak. In an instant, the cat's entrance confused the opponent and he withdrew in bewilderment. With dampened fur, Scooter and Ginger watched the rascal flee as quickly as he had come.

43

Cat Nip:

Those who have an aversion to cats do themselves no favor.

Paws for Prayer:

Dear God, give me the courage to go to the center of a conflict if you have appointed me as peacemaker. Amen.

"Blessed are the peacemakers, for they will be called sons of God."

Matthew 5:9

Scooter was an ambassador of peace, but it cost him exposure and risk. The common advice to stay out of the middle may not always apply. Mediators must often place themselves at the center of trouble to negotiate peace. Don't always shun involvement. Jumping in the middle may hasten a peace.

Cat Tip:

A common injury sustained in cat fights is a bite that becomes infected and abscesses. Signs of an abscess are soft swelling on the limbs or elsewhere, and areas that are tender and painful to the touch. Pus forms under the skin of an abscess. Visit the veterinarian for treatment.

The Tail End:

There never was a good war, or a bad peace.

— Benjamin Franklin

Be Finicky About Your Choice of Words

"Restrict the use of your tongue to grooming, licking, and lapping."

46

Goldie

"Stop, stop, Goldie! You're hurting me!" Michelle winced as she pushed her Abyssinian, Goldie, away from her face. Suddenly her words stung her conscience. She felt sure her caustic remark had hurt Goldie far more than Goldie's sandpaper-like licks had hurt her. Michelle pulled Goldie close to her face for an eye to eye discussion.

"Goldie, the only trouble your tongue ever causes you is an occasional scolding from me for your amorous licks; I wish my tongue was as innocent." Michelle was remorseful. She remembered how her sharp tongue had lashed at a saleswoman earlier that day. She headed for her desk and began a note of apology to the saleslady.

Ever said something unkind and afterwards wished you had held your tongue? The tongue can be a brutal tool at humankind's disposal. Sharp words are known to provoke cries like Michelle's. "Stop, stop! You're hurting me!" At best, the tongue can impart love, courage, and strength by words of affirmation. At worst, the tongue can cause irreparable injury by demeaning words from superiors and peers.

Though Goldie's licks were uncomfortable, Michelle understood Goldie's goodwill. Anyone who has restrained a cat from sustained licking, remembers the scraping sensation of each well-intentioned swipe. The papillae projections on a cat's tongue are designed to wash, comb, cleanse, and lap. Then why

Cat Nip:

If we could talk to the animals, the longest waiting line would be for audience with the cat.

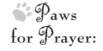

Paws for Prayer:

Dear God, I commit my tongue to You. May I strive to speak only words that encourage. Amen.

"If any man offend not in word, the same is a perfect man."
James 3:2 KJV

48

have catty remarks come to mean comments which are cruel, spiteful, or malicious? To associate such cruelty with a cat's tongue is not an accurate metaphor.

The feline tongue cleanses — help a friend clean up a messy life. The feline tongue combs — assist a colleague untangle a difficult situation. The feline tongue speeds healing — make your life a balm for some wounded heart. A last lick should set people on their feet, not send them to the floor with a blow.

Cat Tip:

Less than five percent of lost cats brought to animal shelters are reunited with their owners. Outfit your cat with an I.D. collar tag for as little as $5.00 and a permanent microchip for around $35.00. The rice-size microchip bearing the cat's identification number is implanted by an injection under the skin at the back of the cat's neck. The chip can be detected by scanners available at veterinarian clinics and animal shelters. Cats with microchips wear a collar tag bearing an 800 phone number for people to call who are attempting to reunite the cat with the owner.

The Tail End:

Give me the ready hand rather than the ready tongue.

— Giuseppe Garibaldi

Everyone Supervises Someone

"Be a wise and winsome watch-cat."

50

Ellie's cats never lose their intrigue with Ellie's nightly routine. All five cats situate themselves shoulder to shoulder in a line on the counter top to watch Ellie step into her deep water bath for a hot and soapy soak.

One day, Ellie called a plumber to repair the bathtub faucet. When the cats heard the running water, they flocked to the bathroom. One, two, three, four, and at last the fifth cat, made the effortless bound to the countertop. The cats undoubtedly presumed the plumber was about to take a plunge. When he reached for his wrench on the vanity top, his gaze met ten yellow eyes supervising his every move. A bit unnerved, he called for Ellie. With forced smile he asked, "Are they tame?"

"Oh yes. They just like to supervise everything that goes on." One of the five jumped down and peeked over the edge of the tub. Another cat headed for the tool chest to sniff the shiny tools. The longer the plumber lingered, the more they scrutinized his work. Reluctantly, he shoved the cats aside while whispering under his breath, "Even my boss isn't this picky."

He completed the repairs — but not without a lot of supervision. As he gathered his tools and prepared to leave, one of the five looked up and meowed. "Good job!" Ellie interpreted. He had already warmed up a little to the furry assistants, but the feline farewell prompted an appreciative smile. The plumber left with a new attitude about cats and supervisors — they only intend to help.

51

Cat Nip:

There are over sixty million cats in the United States. Cats have surpassed dogs in popularity, most likely because they can be happily maintained indoors, and are affectionate and clean.

Paws for Prayer:

Dear God, make me a faithful worker and a wise supervisor. Amen.

"Always remember that you, too, have a Master in heaven who is closely watching you."
Colossians 4:1 TLB

52

Never resent a supervisor. Though they possess the authority to command, they also bear the responsibility for the people and products under their care. Someone looking over your shoulder might make you feel self-conscious, but levels of authority provide an effective safeguard of checks and balances. Mothers watch over children, bosses oversee employees, mayors rule over cities. Try relaxing under the watchful eye of those responsible for your success!

Cat Tip:

Give each of your cats an individual feeding and water bowl. The bowls can be made of anything from stainless steel to pottery. Don't use bowls that slide across the floor or are very deep. The cat that eats only dry food will require a greater intake of water than the cat who gets moisture from canned diets.

The Tail End:

What a fellow lacks in vision somebody must furnish in supervision.

— *Swanson Newsette*

Faith Surmounts the Highest Peaks

*"Nothing is im-paws-sible
with God."*

Hilda, a stray calico, has become a legendary mountain climber for repeatedly scaling the Swiss Alps. In 1928, the adventuresome cat began tagging along with climbers who trekked from the Swiss town of Kandersteg to the nearby mountain of Blumlisalphorn. Finally, she settled for a new home at the 9,000-foot level. It was a mountaineer club's shelter where she was fed by the guard.

Not disposed to abiding on plateaus, Hilda believed she was capable of higher pursuits. One day, she followed a group of climbers ascending to the 12,038-foot peak. To their amazement, she accompanied the group all the way to the summit. At some points along the way, the climbers found it necessary to carry her, but only because it was obvious she wanted to continue.

From that day on, Hilda was known as Switzerland's mountain climbing cat. Between expeditions, she would sit outside the shelter, waiting for the next team of climbers to arrive. When they began their ascent, Hilda would be climbing among them.[6]

55

Cat Nip:

Given a group of nine cat lovers and one cat hater, the cat unfailingly selects the lap of the cat hater for his evening sit.

Paws for Prayer:

Dear God, open my ears to hear and my heart to respond to Your highest calls. Amen.

"With God all things are possible."
Matthew 19:26

Insuperable heights can be achieved by God's enablement. Through faith in Him, exploits which might not be accomplished naturally can be accomplished supernaturally. Like Hilda, goal seekers may need help from fellow climbers when snowstorms strike and ascents are steep. But with God, no aspiration is im-paws-sible.

Cat Tip:

There are two reasons why cat fights escalate when a female is in heat. The male courter may be crossing the boundaries of another cat's territory and provoke a fight, or the female may not be ready to consent to the male contending for her and resist in a fight.

The Tail End:

At the summit of every noble human endeavor, you will find a steeple pointing toward God.

— *Dr. Mack Stokes*

Secrets Are for Keeps

"Don't pass on a confidence without purr-mission."

Wilbur, a lovely British short-hair, was born in medieval England. On his way home by a new route through the market district, a frightening incident occurred. An unshaven man with big hands and offensive breath grabbed Wilbur and

58

stuffed him in a sack. Wilbur then endured a dizzying whirl as the swine merchant twisted the open end of the sack and spun it closed. Wilbur squirmed in an attempt to escape but quickly realized he was trapped in the rude enclosure.

Wilbur then listened to a brief conversation that followed. A brusque client demanded, "A pig, I'll buy." Wilbur felt himself lifted up as the sack was handed to the buyer. "I'll inspect my pig," declared the buyer. When the prospective buyer opened the sack, Wilbur saw his chance and leapt from the bag with a shattering "MEOW."

The shady seller was caught in his deception. Harsh words were exchanged between the two men as Wilbur flashed down the street. He fled amid the clamor of the crowd, determined never again to traverse the market route.

59

Cat Nip:

Nothing attracts cat pawprints to an automobile faster than a fresh wax job or a warm hood.

🐾 Paws for Prayer:

Dear God, help me go beyond the keeping of a secret; teach me to tactfully halt the unpermitted telling of a secret. Amen.

"A talebearer reveals secrets, but he who is of a faithful spirit conceals a matter."

Proverbs 11:13 NKJV

This tale of the dishonest practice of deceiving pig buyers with large cats was how the expression, "Don't let the cat out of the bag" came to mean, "Don't divulge a secret." To disclose a secret is as underhanded as swine merchants who deceived their buyers. Those who faithfully keep a confidence are rare individuals, because the pride of knowing the secret is a great temptation to tell. Don't yield! Disclosing secrets breaks trust and fractures relationships. Be a faithful and trustworthy family member, friend, and employee.

🐾 Cat Tip:

The duration of your cat's confinement in a car during outings should be limited. Water, even in cars, should be available to the cat at all times. Cats die of heatstroke when left too long in hot cars. Cats confined to rooms without adequate ventilation may also suffer heatstroke. Panting, instability on the feet, sweating through the pads, unusual salivation, and general anxiety may indicate heatstroke.

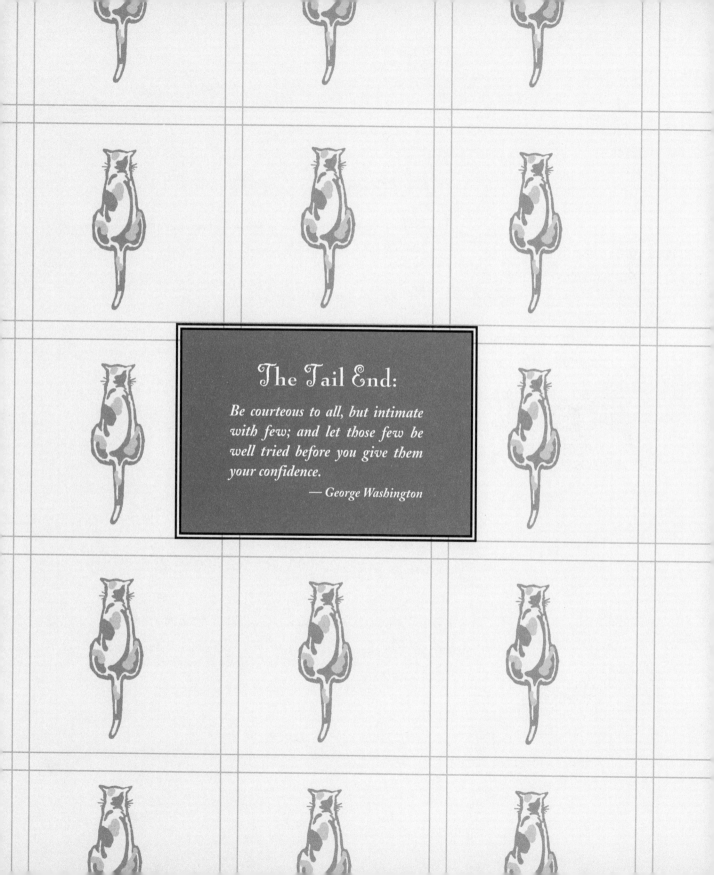

The Tail End:

Be courteous to all, but intimate with few; and let those few be well tried before you give them your confidence.

— George Washington

Dreams Can Come True

"If you're chasing a dream,
don't stop until you cat-ch it."

One afternoon when Chip was in a deep sleep, Heather noticed his furry facial expressions tense. His ears twitched and his eyelids fluttered. He even talked in his sleep with soft cries and short squeals, as he often did during his sixteen hours of

62

sleep each day, an average for cats. She chuckled to herself, as his jaws tightened and his whiskers flicked. Chip was dreaming of catching a skittering mouse or a fluttering bird.

Then a thought struck her. The mice and fowl cat-ches on Heather's back porch proved that cats were not merely dreamers; they made their dreams come true. For ten years, Heather harbored a dream of operating her own home business. Maybe it was time she took a lesson from Chip.

When she shared her desire with a friend, the reaction was not what she expected. "Only in your dreams," the listener said flatly. But Heather was not dissuaded by the deflating response. She remembered once hearing, "Dreams come true by what you do when you're awake, not by what you envision while you sleep."

Heather began the work of launching her business. She consulted a banker, bought supplies, designed brochures, studied manuals, and acquired her first clients. At last, she was in business at home. When her first check came in, she bought their favorite treats and celebrated. "Thanks Chip," she said softly as she handed him a delightful morsel. "The dream I

Cat Nip:

Of cartoon fame are Tom the cat (formerly named Jasper) and Jerry the mouse, (originally unnamed). The film stars made their debut in 1940 under the title, "Puss Gets the Boot." In 1993, they appeared in a full-length movie called Tom and Jerry: The Movie.

Paws for Prayer:

Dear God, give me plausible dreams and spare me from nightmares. Amen.

"At Gibeon the LORD appeared to Solomon in a dream by night; and God said, 'Ask! What shall I give you?'"
1 Kings 3:5 NKJV

64

clutched in my heart all these years of commuting from home to job has come true — thanks to your example!"

If an aspiration appears in your dreams, purr-haps it is yearning for fulfillment. Don't sleep on it! Wake up, work hard, and be your own cat-alyst for making your dreams come true.

Cat Tip:

The folklore that holds a Maine Coon is the offspring of a cat who mated with a raccoon (Coon) is biologically impossible. The Maine Coon breed was likely developed by the mating of American farm cats with Turkish long-hairs brought to Maine in the 19th century by American seamen.

The Tail End:

The faculty to dream was not given to mock us. There is a reality back of it. There is a divinity behind our legitimate desires.

— *Orison Swett Marden*

Tenacity — The Grit of Conviction

"Never budge on the important things."

Tenacity was the runt in a pureblood litter of Seal Point Siamese kittens. Her tiny tail resembled a snip of fuzzy sisal, and her triangular head was oversized for her wee body. A dissonant wail and razor sharp teeth added to this little spectacle of fortitude. Her miniature blue eyes aroused affection and won over Sally and her loving family. In the years to come, they would discover that this imperious kitten was an indomitable fur ball of strength.

Tenacity displayed her strong will as early as her first car ride from the breeder to her new home. She began her iron paw rule by resisting confinement in the box where Sally's husband placed her for the short ride. Her next demonstration of willfulness was to snub the family German Shepherd. From the first day at her new home, she was unyielding about her preferences (dry food only), her sentiments (repugnance for dogs), and her convictions (don't budge on the important things).

Tenacity's most astounding exhibition of invincibility occurred when she was seventeen years old. Following an encounter with an unknown contender who broke her ribs and severed her tail, she staunchly refused even death and recovered — living to the age of twenty-four!

66

Cat Nip:

When a cat insists, who resists?

Paws for Prayer:

Dear God, when it would be easier to relax my stand for what is right, grant me the courage to remain firm. Amen.

"I have set the LORD always before me; because he is at my right hand, I shall not be moved."

Psalm 16:8 KJV

In an era when flexibility and tolerance are exalted, there are still issues that demand immovability. Holding firmly to tenets of faith and persuasions of the heart calls for tenacity. When hope, safety, or morality are threatened, tenacity is indeed a virtue.

Cat Tip:

Over 50 percent of cats favor the use of one paw, with twice as many favoring the left paw as the right one. Perhaps the slang baseball term "southpaw," used for left-handed people, was derived from studies of cats.

The Tail End:

Never, never, never, never give in.

— *Winston Churchill*

Affirm Someone Every Day

*"Rubbing people the <u>right</u> way is
a great method for showing affection."*

Hiss 'n Spit

Hiss 'n Spit is the name our family christened an orange neighborhood cat who often appears on our back porch. Whoever is first to notice his arrival calls the rest of the family together. His peculiar behavior both bewilders and delights us. His combination of vacillating emotions is a strange mix.

He begins his greeting with a firm rub against the nearest knee, and then alternates with hissing, purring, growling, or meowing. His intermittent rubs are the best gesture in his repertoire. Walking in figure eights, he breaks his stride often to give his affectionate rubs. His script of noises may then shift between hissing displeasure and purring delight. My son's assessment is, "Pretty weird cat, Mom."

When Hiss 'n Spit arrives, we try to remember that amidst his growling, spitting, and groaning is the welcome purring, plus a lot of affirming rubs that make his visits worthwhile. We all agree that his frequent caresses are worth tolerating his other sentiments.

We have learned from Hiss 'n Spit how helpful it is to affirm one another with encouraging words and warm hugs. Though we have moments in our family when any one of us might hiss or growl, we seem to recover more quickly when we extend affection to each other.

69

Cat Nip:

When a cat sits with both feet tucked inward and studies you with the same admiration you would direct toward a Rembrandt, you know you have been adopted.

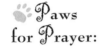

Paws for Prayer:

Dear God, give me grace to accept love from others, and to extend it to those in need, even when I'm struggling with trials of my own. Amen.

"Love one another. As I have loved you, so you must love one another."
John 13:34

70

The journey of life is marked with emotions as varied as a cat's. Living through mixed joys and assorted sorrows, people gain strength by giving and receiving approbation along the way. When days are punctuated with pauses for affection, those who give are renewed and those who receive are strengthened.

Cat Tip:

Corporal punishment is not a good method for disciplining cats. Instead, shake the finger in front of the cat's nose and say loudly, "No!" A spritz of water from a spray bottle is another harmless and often helpful method of correction. Clapping the hands sharply or shaking an aluminum can filled with pennies will also discourage a cat's unapproved actions.

The Tail End:

Lavish (love) upon the poor, where it is very easy; especially upon the rich, who often need it most; most of all upon our equals, where it is very difficult.

— Henry Drummond

The Great Tutor of Experience

"It is folly to take a second lap of sour milk."

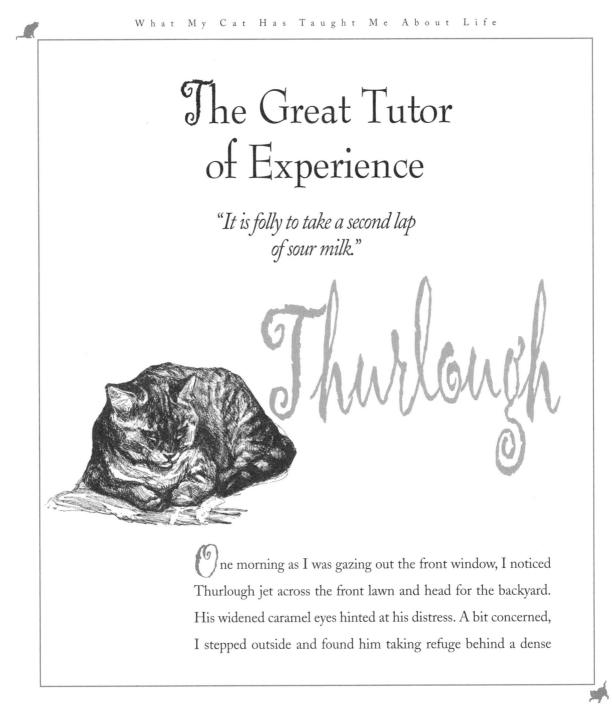

One morning as I was gazing out the front window, I noticed Thurlough jet across the front lawn and head for the backyard. His widened caramel eyes hinted at his distress. A bit concerned, I stepped outside and found him taking refuge behind a dense shrub. I scooped him up and carried him to his favorite nap site at the foot of our bed.

When the doorbell rang a few minutes later, I opened upon a pale and saddened neighbor. She announced haltingly, "I think I drove over your cat." I realized at that moment that Thurlough had come close to an early cat-acomb.

"Well, if you did he has recovered remarkably fast. I just brought him inside and he's asleep on my bed," I explained. We both had reason to smile.

My sensitive neighbor sighed with relief. "He darted in front of my car and rolled out of sight; I couldn't avoid him. But he wasn't caught under the tires." We examined him, and other than an overly sensitive tail, he seemed unharmed. After discussing the mishap, we were optimistic that Thurlough had not been injured.

Prior to Thurlough's loud and frightful introduction to the underside of a four by four, he frequently crossed the busy arterial nearby. The mouse field across the street lured his pursuits. But Thurlough was a learner. After that day six years ago, he never crossed again. I saw him trace the golf course, walk the curb top,

73

 Cat Nip:

Kittens are like clowns, clad in striped suits.

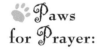

Paws for Prayer:

Dear God, don't let me waste the pain of a bad experience by the foolhardiness of repeating it. Amen.

"Fools despise wisdom and instruction."
Proverbs 1:7 NASB

74

and visit neighbors to the west and the east of us. But busy Perry Street was off Thurlough's limits — by his own prudent choice!

Even the cautious cat is sometimes careless and pays the price of a dangerous encounter. Everyone makes mistakes, but to err twice on the same matter is a deliberate choice to fail. To *learn* from error is the reward of experience.

Cat Tip:

Milk and cream can cause diarrhea in cats. It is suspected cats lack the enzyme necessary to break down lactose in the stomach. Some cats are not bothered by a few teaspoons diluted with water, given on an occasional basis.

The Tail End:

Experience is a wonderful thing; it enables you to recognize a mistake every time you make it!

— Heartland Samplers, Inc.

Never Stamp Out Hope

"Being present is sometimes all that's needed to impart hope."

"Watch out! That cat is a terror!" Those seven words of warning were Dee's introduction to the calico mother at the animal shelter where Dee volunteered. Realizing the mother cat and her four kittens were indeed terrorized by their strange and threatening environment, Dee took them home to foster temporarily.

The cat remained hostile in the Sheppe home, where she had to cohabit with Dee's two sons, two other cats, and a cat-friendly dog. When the kittens were old enough to adopt, Dee returned the mother and her litter to the shelter. Soon the kittens were adopted, but their mother had grown ill and was still homeless. Dee took the hapless cat home and nursed her back to health before returning her to the shelter for a third time.

Soon after, the shelter called again, this time giving an ultimatum. The incorrigible cat was wailing incessantly and was disruptive in her cage. Dee rescued her again and drove her to the veterinarian to be spayed. When the vet asked the cat's name, Dee exclaimed in despair, "I don't know. She's hopeless!" Suddenly, a thought struck. The cat had escaped the shelter three times. Hopeless? Not so. The cat's name became obvious. The name Hope was recorded on her chart. Hope settled into the Sheppe household and became their most affectionate pet.

One day, Dee's teenage son suffered a major disappointment. He sat alone with his head drooping for over an hour. Hope

Cat Nip:

A group of lions is called a pride. A group of domestic cats is called a clowder.

Paws for Prayer:

Dear God, when I am despondent, remind me that hope waits for me to grasp hold. Amen.

"Be strong and take heart, all you who hope in the LORD."

Psalm 31:24

waited at his feet. Dee grew panicky as she watched her son's struggle. Finally he stood up and almost stepped on Hope. He looked at Dee and smiled confidently, "I'm okay, Mom. I almost stamped out Hope, but I'm okay."

The Sheppe family now encourages anyone who feels hopeless with this prudent admonition — "Never stamp out Hope."

Cat Tip:

Providing your cat with a bed should be a simple and inexpensive project. A cardboard box large enough for the cat to stretch out and lined with a soft blanket is adequate. Place the bed away from drafts and high traffic areas. Wash the blanket monthly to kill flea eggs and remove fur. Cats sometimes prefer a high place for their bed.

The Tail End:

Hope is the parent of faith.

— *Cyrus A. Bartol*

Perseverance — The Push of Pursuit

*"If something is worth chasing,
don't stop until it's captured."*

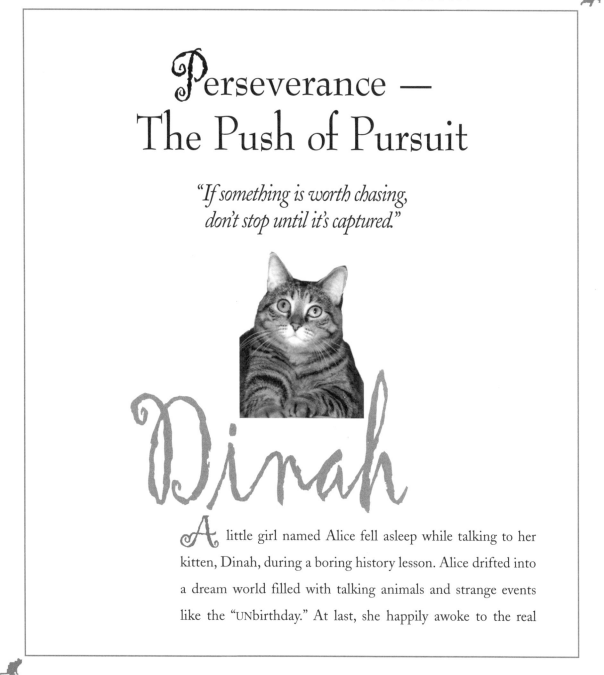

A little girl named Alice fell asleep while talking to her kitten, Dinah, during a boring history lesson. Alice drifted into a dream world filled with talking animals and strange events like the "UNbirthday." At last, she happily awoke to the real world and to Dinah, who meowed rather than talked — like the Cheshire Cat Alice encountered in her dream.

Alice met the crazed but clever Cheshire Cat as she traveled through a nonsensical wonderland where flowers sang and rabbits wore waistcoats. The English Cheshire Cat was always smiling with a mischievous, wide, and toothy grin. He was capable of vanishing and reappearing, of twisting his head upside down, and accomplishing other incredulous acts. At one point in Alice's journey, she was perplexed about which fork in the road to take. To help her, the Cheshire Cat asked her where she wanted to go. Alice hadn't a clue where she was headed and so she explained — "so long as I get *somewhere*...."

"Oh, you're sure to do that," said the cat, "if you only walk long enough!" His recommendation to "just keep walking" was the one sensible thing Alice heard from the wildly fantastic creatures in her dream.

Cat Nip:

Politically correct alley cats prefer to be called "random bred."

80

Paws for Prayer:

Dear God, when I feel like giving up, help me keep the end in sight. Amen.

"Let us not become weary in doing good; for at the proper time we will reap a harvest if we do not give up."

Galatians 6:9

Alice, of course, is the main character of *Alice in Wonderland*, the classic story by Lewis Carroll. Her adventure illustrates that pursuing a goal to the end requires perseverance — the discipline of continuing, the fortitude to press on, and the faithfulness to finish. The journey may be so difficult at times that it seems surreal. In a sometimes insane world, the best and only course is to simply trudge on.

Cat Tip:

Some common indoor plants which cats *should not* chew include: asparagus, fern, avocado, azalea, buttercup, creeping Charlie, Dieffenbachia (can be fatal), dumb cane, Easter lily, elephant ear, English ivy, iris, cherry laurel, lily of the valley, mistletoe, morning glory, oleander, philodendron, poinsettia, rhubarb, and yew.

The Tail End:

Consider the postage stamp, my son. It secures success through its ability to stick to one thing till it gets there.

— *Josh Billings*

*L*ove Eases the Stress of Patience

"Patience endures because it is motivated by love."

Fluffy

The Owl and the Pussycat were an odd couple in literature's animal kingdom. As they sailed away in their pea green boat, the owl crooned his love to the pussycat, while strumming his guitar. The pussycat responded to her "elegant fowl" with the suggestion that they marry. Their mutual affection was indisputable.

Such is the affection between a cockatiel and a Persian belonging to my neighbors, the Danielsons. Among their two exotic birds and two Persian cats, there is no question which species is boss — the birds! But their dominance has not quelled the cats' affection for the birds.

Fluffy, a shaded silver Persian, is a true comrade to Sunny, the cockatiel. One wintry afternoon, Sunny discovered the backside of the refrigerator was a warm place and he decided to linger. When the Danielsons noticed Sunny was missing, they began a search for him, looking in all the usual undersides and corners and calling out, "Sunny! Where are you, Sunny?"

Thirty minutes of hunting in vain left the Danielsons frustrated and concerned. Preoccupied with Sunny, they had overlooked Fluffy's clue. She had stood beside the refrigerator, unmoved from her watch, expecting the family to see Sunny, only inches away from her. At last, they took notice of Fluffy's quiet mewing and found the cocky cockatiel behind the humming appliance.

83

Cat Nip:

Def-fur-nition of fur-ment: Too many cats in a household.
— Jeanne Bjornsen

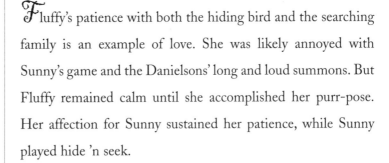

Paws for Prayer:

Dear God, I know I add stress to tense situations when I respond impatiently. Remind me to ask for your patience at such times. Amen.

"Be patient with everyone."
1 Thessalonians 5:14

*F*luffy's patience with both the hiding bird and the searching family is an example of love. She was likely annoyed with Sunny's game and the Danielsons' long and loud summons. But Fluffy remained calm until she accomplished her purr-pose. Her affection for Sunny sustained her patience, while Sunny played hide 'n seek.

Cat Tip:

A once-a-month oral flea control product for cats is now available. The suspension is contained in a small pouch which is mixed with canned food, tuna oil, or a moist treat. To cure an *adult* flea infestation already present, use another treatment in conjunction. Within several weeks adult fleas will die and the suspension will prevent immature fleas from developing.

The Tail End:

Adopt the pace of nature; her secret is patience.

—*Emerson*

Opportunity Waits for the Watchful

*"Don't miss a chance to get
your paw in the door."*

Kitten

When Christine's neighbor brought home a new cat, Christine acquired a new cat too — the same one, in fact. The powder gray kitten soon became an artist at subtle entries into Christine's house. "He knows every access," Christine told me.

"He slips in when I open the front door to salespersons or step out the back door to shake a rug. Once he ran in when I shooed a fly past the screen door. Every morning when I step out to the porch and reach for the newspaper, I collide with that kitten."

"Kitten" exercises cunning prowess in maneuvering between and around Christine's legs. In the split second needed to identify the darting gray movement, he's already inside. "I'm beginning to suspect the wind itself helps blow him in," said Christine. "When it's chilly outdoors, he is extra clever at assessing any occasion to enter. And what's cute is this," she said. "Though he's unobtrusive when sneaking in, once indoors he makes his appearance openly. His wiggling tail tip implies, 'Well, I'm here. Now what shall we play?'"

Kitten's success at admitting himself is not merely fortuitous. He has paid a lot of attention to the activity around Christine's house to learn where, when, and how to get inside. When everything is right, he moves swiftly. Seldom does he miss his chance.

87

Cat Nip:

The smallest feline is a masterpiece.
— Leonardo da Vinci

Paws for Prayer:

Dear God, help me be patient as I look for opportunity, and give me courage to move forward when it comes my way. Amen.

"Devote yourselves to prayer, being watchful and thankful."
Colossians 4:2

88

Don't mistake opportunity with luck. Good fortune can fall to anyone, but opportunity comes to those who are prepared, determined, and watching patiently for a door to open. At the sound of a turning knob, look for a crack in the doorway. Then move hastily. Op-purr-tunities abound. Be ready to poise your paw in the door before it is closed.

Cat Tip:

Spraying is the way cats mark their territory. Indoor cats should be neutered between five and six months of age *before* spraying becomes a habit difficult to break. Reasons cats begin spraying include a feeling of threat regarding their territory, stress caused by routine changes (a move, a new baby, home remodeling), or lastly, the presence of an in-season female.

The Tail End:

When opportunity knocks at the door some people are out in the back yard looking around for four-leaf clovers.
— *Vaughn Monroe*

Beware of Jealousy

"Jealousy prompts excessive rivalry and can cause some purr-ty bad behavior."

Marmalade

"Marmalade, are you going to be polite tonight?" Marmalade's jealous disposition surfaced when Katherine began dating after her husband passed away. Katherine noticed that Marmalade was not fond of her new suitor. When the gentleman escorted Katherine out for the evening, Marmalade felt temporarily deserted. Thus, she did all she could to discourage Katherine's social outings.

The new visitor was given a swift swat against the heel with a swing from Marmalade's carefully aimed paw. Her rude tactic was clearly an attempt to dissuade Katherine's courting. Then Marmalade's conduct grew worse. Failing to distinguish between Katherine's evening male suitor and the daytime male servicemen, Marmalade began swatting the heels of everyone.

Orange-fur Marmalade was battling green-eyed jealousy, so Katherine decided to dispel Marmalade's fears of rejection. The next time he called for her, Katherine took a moment to introduce Marmalade to her new friend. The caller offered a gentle pet and a firm stroke across the kitty's soft head. Thus Marmalade soon formed a new idea about sundown suitors — they came to give affection. Marmalade is swatting less and purring more. She's losing her fear of being supplanted and is learning to be paw-lite.

Cat Nip:

In order of high frequency hearing acuity, these four mammals rate accordingly, with the cat hearing less than each of the other three listed: porpoises, bats, mice, cats.

Paws for Prayer:

Dear Lord, where my love is strongest, I am prone to jealousy. Help me keep a pure heart and a level head to prevent the ugly strife of rivalry. Amen.

"Jealousy is the rage of a man."

Proverbs 6:34 KJV

Jealousy is often irrational, because it conjectures offenses. It surfaces when a person feels threatened. Totally self-absorbed, jealousy whines with complaints that always begin with "I." "I wasn't asked, I wasn't chosen, I wasn't invited." It discolors attitude and provokes rude affronts, and it should be recognized quickly and confessed. The only fruit of jealousy is misery.

Cat Tip:

Some white cats have one green eye and one blue eye. Deafness is an anomaly in some blue-eyed white cats.

The Tail End:

Jealousy, (is) the jaundice of the soul.

— *John Dryden*

91

Forgiveness Brings Warmth

*"Forgiving is harder than
finding a good home."*

Myles

Myles was fightin' mad! He arrived at our home twenty-
four hours after his two siblings, Earl and Murray. All three
kittens had been neutered and were waiting at the veterinary
clinic, but we had arranged to bring home only two. Myles was

returned to his foster home, while Earl and Murray came home with us. The separation was tough for Myles, and recovering from surgery without Earl and Murray was even worse.

I was the dissenter who thought three kittens was one too many, but the following day I reconsidered. My husband's appeal to "keep the brothers together" finally weakened my resolve. Ecstatic, he hurried to the phone to arrange for the adoption of Myles.

Presuming the kitten reunion would be a happy event, we were anxious to reunite the three brothers. Contrary to our expectations, Myles spat, hissed, swatted, and refused the welcome from Earl and Murray. We were bewildered, until we remembered he was recovering from the discomfort of surgery and his temporary rejection. The introduction to strange surroundings did not help his mood.

That first evening was tense for everyone. Myles declined invitations from his brothers to playful wrestling and huddled by himself in an obvious furor of unforgiveness. "Poor little fellow," commented my husband, "I guess he wants someone to blame."

93

Cat Nip:

"No matter how much cats fight, there always seems to be plenty of kittens."
—*Abraham Lincoln*

🐾 Paws for Prayer:

Dear God, when my emotions oppose my willingness to forgive, help me to forgive with my will. Amen.

"Bear with each other and forgive whatever grievances you may have against one another. Forgive as the Lord forgave you."
Colossians 3:13

The next morning we were relieved to find Myles sleeping in a furry pile between his siblings. Apparently he decided that blaming was not much fun and being together again was what he wanted all along. Forgiving his brothers for their temporary desertion made his night warmer and the new day brighter.

🐾   🐾   🐾

There are no platitudes asserting that forgiveness is easy. It is perhaps the hardest moral act humans accomplish. Only the magnitude of God's forgiveness toward us can inspire and enable us to forgive those who hurt and harm us.

🐾 Cat Tip:

Fresh air and outdoor scents are possible for cats within the limits of a safe environment. Provide a small ledge inside a screen window, place a table designated for the cat near a screen window, or build an outdoor enclosure with a run leading in and out of the house. Some owners install a sliding glass door which can be opened to a screen door. Keep screens in repair.

The Tail End:

He that cannot forgive others breaks the bridge over which he must pass himself; for every man has need to be forgiven.

— Thomas Fuller

The Joy of Generosity

"Give lavishly."

Omari

96

Only a cat lover like Roger Caras would take kindly to an array of sticks and an occasional gift of horse manure strewn on his porches daily. Orange and white Omari is his feline retriever. "Omari, often looking for all the world like George Burns with his cigar, brings us sticks," writes Caras, president of the American Society for the Prevention of Cruelty to Animals. Omari delivers to the house several dozen one- to six-inch lengths of wooden treasures a day. They must be swept away, lest they become a stumbling hazard blocking the doorway.

Most cats deliver captured mice or birds to their owners, but Caras says sticks are Omari's "thing." It is Omari's generosity that makes any scolding about his stick fetish seem out of the question. What Omari does, he does wholeheartedly. Though his gifts are an oddity, they are nonetheless gifts offered in abundance.[7]

One theory explaining why cats bring rodents and birds to their owners is that they are mimicking how they teach their kittens to catch and eat small prey. Since human companions are regarded as the cat's family, cats feel compelled to teach humans the skills of the kill. Owners are usually not enamored with gifts of preyed-upon victims. But remembering the "thought behind it" helps humans transcend the barrier between human and feline practice.

97

🐾 Cat Nip:

Heading into a real screaming cat brawl can be like grabbing a spinning circular saw.
— Roger A. Caras

Paws for Prayer:

Dear God, help me to be willing to give joyfully, whether my gift be modest or extravagant. Amen.

"Let each one do just as he has purposed in his heart; not grudgingly or under compulsion; for God loves a cheerful giver."

2 Corinthians 9:7 NASB

Generous giving is a joyful act. Add liberality to every gift. Order an appetizer with your gift of lunch. Tie a token present to the outside of a package. Include a bookmark with a book, a card of earrings with a blouse, a snapshot with a letter, a candy bar with a birthday card, or an extra 10 percent to a donation. The extra can transform a customary gift into an unforgettable delight.

Cat Tip:

The best response to a cat's gift of killed prey is to speak words of praise and then stroke the kitty for his or her efforts. While the cat is not watching, dispose of the deceased critter.

The Tail End:

Generosity is measured not by the size of the gift, but by the size of the store that remains.

Everybody Deserves To Be Rescued

"Never ignore a cry for help."

Pouncer

Pouncer was abandoned in an attic for three months, barely surviving on mice. The starving and dehydrated four-pound cat was taken to the Humane Society by the owners of the house. Evidently, the previous renters had deserted her. Her lifesavers were met with Pouncer's swinging paws, needle-sharp claws, and repeated hisses. "She did all a cat can do to resist her rescue," the landlord told the society worker.

When my friend Mary Ann arrived at the Humane Society to acquire a cat, she stated plainly, "We need the best mouser you've got. Our landscape business is threatened by a mouse population that's eating our grass seed faster than we can plant it." The Animal Care Technician pointed to Pouncer. "She's the one you want, and we'll be more than happy to adopt her out." Pouncer lay alone on a small round rug, brooding her past and lashing her tail. She had regained her lost weight and had been spayed. Mary Ann could hardly believe the long-haired, blue eyed cat with the soft Siamese colors was a "working cat."

After hearing the cat's history, Mary Ann bundled up Pouncer and unrolled her into a carrier. With rancorous objection to her second rescue, Pouncer fastened her teeth on Mary Ann's fingers as she closed the latch on the carrier. "Ow!" Mary Ann yelped. As they drove away, she realized the cat's earlier deprivation had turned her into a despicable little animal.

Cat Nip:

Kittens are always a-mew-sing.

Paws for Prayer:

Dear God, don't let me judge a person's worth before launching a rescue. Amen.

"He (God) rescues and He saves."
Daniel 6:27

The company guard dog was next to confront Pouncer's pluck. Upon their introduction, the German Shepherd's nose received a lacerating rake from Pouncer's brown paw. Nevertheless, Pouncer rapidly cleaned out the robber rodents. Though her temperament did not soften, she seemed to realize she was needed, whether she was liked or not.

Mary Ann admits that she and Pouncer have become friends. The other employees refer to Pouncer as "your cat." When I asked Mary Ann if she had a moral to Pouncer's story, she summarized it clearly: "Even the despicable are worth a rescue."

Cat Tip:

Dry cat food adds an abrasive action during chewing that helps prevent the buildup of tartar on a cat's teeth. But an added amount of canned food will in no way be a deterrent to your cat's oral heath. Choose labels on both dry and canned food that note "complete and balanced nutrition."

The Tail End:

Believe me, every man has his secret sorrows, which the world knows not; and oftimes we call a man cold, when he is only sad.
— *Henry Wadsworth Longfellow*

Anger Isn't Always Bad

"Hissing is sometimes appropriate."

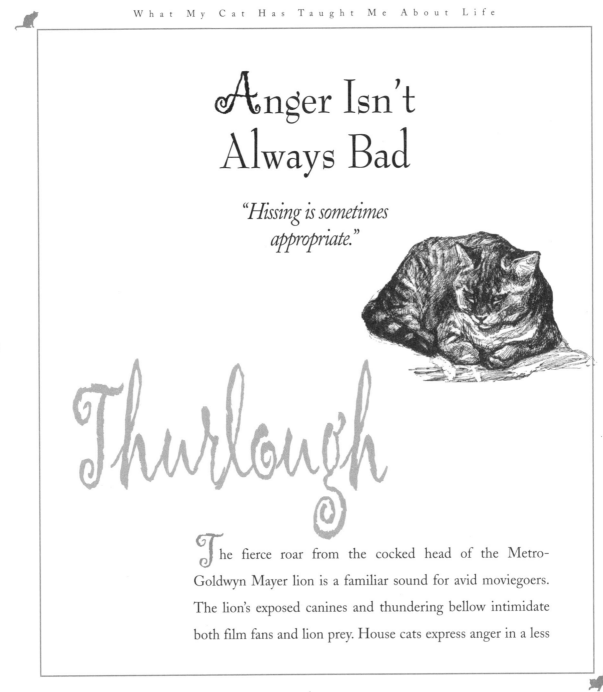

104

Thurlough

The fierce roar from the cocked head of the Metro-Goldwyn Mayer lion is a familiar sound for avid moviegoers. The lion's exposed canines and thundering bellow intimidate both film fans and lion prey. House cats express anger in a less demonstrative manner by flattening their ears and hissing softly.

One day Thurlough, my orange and white tabby, quietly ate from his copper food bowl. Suddenly, he was caught in the volley of an argument between my son and me. Thurlough interrupted our exchange of harsh words with a hiss of outrage. I was so amused by his catty reaction, my angry mood vanished. I turned to my son and said through a smile, "Look! Even Thurlough is mad." We burst into laughter.

Though anger has a negative connotation, it is a God-given emotion. Channeled constructively, anger has aroused people from all generations to accomplish positive things. My own ire over my daughter's dangerous toy led me to discard it, thus sparing her a possible injury. Fury over the abandonment of animals, birthed nationwide humane societies which offer temporary shelter for cats and dogs. An organization named M.A.D.D. (Mother's Against Drunk Driving) was formed to legalize responsible action against drunk drivers. Anger isn't always bad.

Cat Nip:

If an adventure becomes too much of an effort, the cat feels no compunction to venture on.

Paws for Prayer:

Dear Lord, help me use my anger as a tool and not a weapon. Amen.

"Better...a man who controls his temper than one who takes a city."

Proverbs 16:32

In a world where anger is often abusive rather than productive, try to be different. Though hissing is sometimes appropriate, avoid the "mad cat" response. It is wiser to express your wrath with controlled growls, not sharp claws.

Cat Tip:

A cat who eats grass is not always ill. Wild carnivores often eat the semi-digested plant material in the stomach of their prey. The domesticated cat also enjoys the natural tonic of an occasional grass salad.

The Tail End:

When I am angry I can write, pray, and preach well, for then my whole temperament is quickened, my understanding sharpened, and all mundane vexations and temptations depart.

— *Martin Luther*

Devotion Is More Than a Prayer

*"Actions speak louder
than meows."*

Thomas

Thomas was surnamed "the church cat." He lived with the Williams family, next door to a small community church. The Williams worshipped at the family church across town, but Thomas chose the congregation within walking distance. He kept no calendar, yet never failed to be present and on time for both Sunday School and church services every Sabbath.

Thomas wanted to serve, but he didn't know where he fit. The Williamses had never dubbed him a talker, so he concluded he would not be the best volunteer for teaching Sunday School. Since he was not gainfully employed, he was not able to contribute to the collection. Thomas could have offered his pest control services but he declined, choosing to honor the church mice who enjoyed their sanctuary in the church crawl space.

The ministry Thomas decided upon came quite naturally. He noticed that each parishioner appreciated his greetings along the walkway leading to the stained glass doors. Their smiles, strokes, and responses of "Good morning, Kitty" assured Thomas he had found a place to serve. Hospitality was a skill he had learned already. At home he greeted all callers with a welcome rub and a high-tailed escort to his front door. Greeting was something he did well, so he offered it to God.

108

Cat Nip:

Swinging pet doors should come with a disclaimer that reads: "If owners are present, cats prefer assisted entrances and exits through people doors."

Paws for Prayer:

Dear God, make me faithful in attendance at worship and ready to express my devotion through service. Amen.

"I rejoiced with those who said to me, 'Let us go to the house of the LORD'."

Psalm 122:1

Thomas got it all right. He did not wait for someone to invite him to church. He selected a house of worship and attended regularly. He filled a place where he was qualified to serve and became a dependable member. Thomas' life was a cat-echism by example.

Cat Tip:

To make handling your cat more tolerable, trim the claws regularly. The degree of sharpness will tell you when a periodic trimming is necessary. Special clippers are available at pet stores to make the job easier. Gently squeeze the paw to expose the claws. Do not cut through the transparent pink area in the claw.

The Tail End:

One thing I know: the only ones among you who will be really happy are those who will have sought and found how to serve.

— *Albert Schweitzer*

Boundaries Signal Privacy

"Respecting boundaries will eliminate major alter-cat-ions."

"You get yourself outta here! Scat, cat!" Emma jumped up from among her beautiful zinnias and grabbed the broom off the porch to rout the intruder. "Bix!" she called over her shoulder to her husband. "That big cat is spraying in my flower beds again!" Emma Bixler was not fond of Sergeant, a transient cat who enforced strict maintenance of his boundaries around the Bixler farm.

Bix was repairing his truck. "Can't come now, Emma."

Sergeant ran a short distance, then turned to face Emma with a look that said, "What is your problem?" Male cats, like Sergeant, claim and patrol territories ten times larger than those of females, and he was simply doing his job.

Mr. Bixler explained to me once, "Emma and I have watched Sergeant establish his perimeters by spraying and urinating at the borders of our property for some time. His ripped ear and scarred tail are visible proof that he defends these borders, too. But Serg keeps the mouse numbers down, so I don't fuss much about him."

Emma grumbles about the feline rivalry they frequently overhear through their bedroom window at night. "Bix and I are all too familiar with the night sound of quarreling cats contesting our property." If an area is not regarded as neutral, trespassing cats can expect rival reactions from the permanent feline resident. Mr. Bixler seems to understand. "Sergeant is

111

Cat Nip:

Def-fur-nition of de-fur: Mutual results of a cat fight.
— Jeanne Bjornsen

Paws for Prayer:

Dear God, forgive me for offenses I have caused by overstepping the sensitive boundaries of others. Amen.

"Each of you should look not only to your own interests, but also to the interests of others."
Philippians 2:4

just doing what comes naturally, so he's a little perplexed when Emma begins her chase with the broom."

People who attempt to "maintain their fences" are sometimes uncordially viewed as sergeant types. Yet, even communities and nations set fixed boundaries which forbid interlopers. Everyone needs a place sanctioned from intruders. Running roughshod over personal boundaries is a wrongful act. Desk name plates, closed doors, and locker padlocks identify locations with limited access. Boundary violations may also be borrowing without asking, attending without an invitation, or even playful teasing. Learn and honor the boundaries of others. Respecting boundaries prevents both cat spats and relationship wrangles.

Cat Tip:

Two ways to discourage visitor cats who scent mark in your yard with their urine and feces are to (1) spot plant marigold flowers, the odor of which is offensive to cats, or (2) apply commercial products on the ground that smell like cat urine and signal the presence of "another cat."

The Tail End:

We learned the first lesson about boundaries when our mothers told us not to pick the tulips from the neighbor's yard.

There's a Good Side of Change

"Shedding the old makes way for the new."

Maggie

114

Things got real hairy around the Smith home this year when Maggie went through her twice yearly molt. Mr. Smith was heard requesting, "Please try to keep Maggie off my recliner; I don't need the extra cushion from her shed fur." The Smith's teenage daughter was heard moaning, "Mom, I left my Homecoming dress on my bed. Maggie slept on it. It's covered with hair!"

Shedding is a normal and purposeful feline process. Dead hairs loosen from the cat's body allowing new hair to grow. In the spring and fall, evidence of Maggie's gray fur is everywhere in the house, particularly noticeable on the oriental rug and on Mr. Smith's black suit legs. Wisps of fur gather on the weather stripping along the door jam, and crisscross designs of hair lodge in the fuzzy leaves of the African Violet. Fur clumps collect under the kitchen stools where Maggie begs for tidbits, and fur clings to the textured wallpaper where she props her ample body.

When Maggie's shed fur began annoying everyone, a few good changes occurred. As Maggie changed her fur coat, the Smiths changed too. Patsy Smith bought lint rollers for each family member and a new vacuum attachment designed for furniture. Their daughter, Crystal, began hanging up her clothes. Mr. Smith volunteered to brush Maggie each evening. All the changes helped. Albeit, Mr. Smith continued mumbling through his moustache, "That cat!"

Cat Nip:

Def-fur-nition of fur-niture: Where it lands.
— Jeanne Bjornsen

115

Paws for Prayer:

Dear God, when I am forced to surrender the ways of the past, help me adapt with compassion, courage, and optimism. Amen.

"Do not dwell on the past. See, I am doing a new thing! Now it springs up; do you not perceive it?"

Isaiah 43:18-19

116

Shedding old ways and adopting new ones is a lifelong process. Older folks are sometimes resistant to change, but youth also struggle in the throes of any alteration. Nevertheless, the passages of change foster growth. So, think positively about change. Regard it instead as an EXchange — the surrender of one thing to gain another. Like Maggie, shake loose of the old and prepare for the new.

Cat Tip:

Comb your short-hair cat with a blunt-toothed comb during the shedding seasons (spring and fall), and finish by smoothing your hands over the cat's fur and gently massaging the skin. Stop the process if static electricity generated by combing begins to irritate the cat. Long-hair cats require daily brushing.

The Tail End:

Things do not change, we do.
    — Henry Thoreau

Counsel Focuses Vision

"When you're feeling as confused as a cross-eyed cat, seek straightforward counsel."

Peepers

Ross Syler woke up Saturday morning with Peepers standing on his chest, staring at him with her beautiful blue crossed eyes. Peeper's perplexed visage made her no less a splendid kitty. She might *look* confused, but Peepers is never confounded.

Peepers' crossed eyes are a common genetic weakness in the Siamese breed, but Ross was facing vision troubles of a different kind. "Peepers, I feel as confused as you look, but you seem to have it together." Peepers gave Ross a lick of comfort and a purr of hope. Ross began to unload on Peepers like a client unloads on a counselor.

"Mom needs more visits; the nurse says she's failing. Janey hinted our marriage is suffering from neglect. And the boss asked everyone on the Task Team to work overtime the next three months." Peepers curled up in a ball. She always knew what to do next, not like Ross these past months.

Ross didn't know *where* to focus. He had too many demands and too little time. The competition of highly important commitments was conflicting. However, he noticed that sharing his problem, even with Peepers, had helped a little. He began to think, *Maybe I need to consult a professional.* Ross was fortunate that his firm staffed a corporate counselor. One session with the advisor, and he received some practical guidance for balancing his life. Peepers is pleased too. Now she is also getting more time with Ross.

Cat Nip:

Def-fur-nition of atmos-fur: Airborne cat hair.
— Jeanne Bjornsen

119

Paws for Prayer:

Dear God, guide me in the careful selection of a sound counselor. Amen.

"Plans fail for lack of counsel, but with many advisers they succeed."

Proverbs 15:22

People sometimes suffer the confusion of clouded vision. Multiple options present an array of choices. When cross-purposes obscure a clear view of solutions, seek the counsel of a sound advisor. Good counsel is objective and impartial. Advisors are so called because they "add vision" to hazy perceptions. Straight advice from a wise counselor will help sharpen your vision.

Cat Tip:

The way a cat's eyes glow at night is called "night shine." A reflection from a mirror in the cat's retina produces the fluorescent quality and occurs when a sudden blaze of light falls upon wide-open pupils that have been in the dark. Though cats cannot see in total darkness, they see in light levels that humans would describe as total darkness.

The Tail End:

Give us clear vision that we may know where to stand and what to stand for, because unless we stand for something, we shall fall for anything.

— *Peter Marshall*

Decorum —
More than Manners

*"Always put your best
paw forward."*

122

Calico Cleo is like a carefully selected household fixture in the Henry home. Even her fur matches the family room color scheme. She blends perfectly with the patchwork pillows, the country print wallpaper, and the colorful braided rug. Not only does Cleo fit the decor, Mrs. Henry says Cleo always conducts herself with the most fitting decorum. She can be counted on to display appropriate behavior at any event.

Cleo puts her best paw forward when Aunt Hattie visits — the relative who prefers dogs over cats. Even Aunt Hattie concedes that Cleo is a *nice* cat. "No deplorable begging at the table, no destructive clawing on the furniture or uninvited leaps into the lap," she praises Cleo.

Cleo's hospitality includes gracious greetings expressed in purring rhapsodies. When guests are present, the conventions of politeness are extra important. To enhance her coif-fur for company, Cleo situates herself in the middle of activity and engages in a thorough washing. With an occasional upward glance she seems to say, "*Do* make yourself comfortable." Cleo's decorum is more than an outward show. She and Mrs. Henry sincerely believe their guests deserve a gracious reception.

 Cat Nip:

Every kitten is mew-nique.

123

Paws for Prayer:

Dear God, whether I am guest or host, make me a welcome presence in any social setting. Amen.

"(Love)...does not behave rudely."

1 Corinthians 13:5 NKJV

124

Decorum has unfairly become associated with snobbery in recent years. Thus, it has become an expected norm only at military academies, private clubs, and formal teas. The fact is, prescribed conduct suits certain affairs in the same manner that swimming trunks suit the beach and a lace gown befits a bride. Fitting in, appropriately nurtures opportunities that impropriety may avert. Conforming to custom also shows respect and sensitivity. Defer to decorum. How you purr-form purr-tains to both ethics and grace.

Cat Tip:

Ferrets, not cats, were kept as mousers in Greece. Interestingly, the Greek word for ferret — ailouros — is the root syllable for the English word, ailurophile, meaning "a cat lover."

The Tail End:

Etiquette means behaving yourself a little better than is absolutely essential.

— *Will Cuppy*

Determination Launches Initiative

*"Get a grip by digging in
with your claws."*

The Rollinses began to think Tuffy was benefiting more than their son, Randy, from all Mr. Rollins' lectures about hard work and determination. Randy was continually behind in his schoolwork, but Tuffy was notorious at digging in. The Rollins'

125

leather couch and wing back chair suffered indescribable abuse, until the Rollinses headed for the pet store and asked for help. "How do you correct a cat that claws the furniture?" The clerk recommended a few repellents, but a patron who overheard their question shared the saving advice.

"We tried everything," said the bystander, "but what worked best was a squirt of water from a spray bottle. Our Charlie hated it. We bought a scratching post and rubbed it with fresh catnip the same night we started the water treatment. We kept the water bottle within reach to use consistently for a couple weeks. Charlie learned quickly that furniture was a 'no paws zone.' To reinforce use of the scratching pole, we rewarded him with kitty treats."

The Rollinses gave it a try. Each time Tuffy dug into a drapery, sofa, or carpet, the spritz of water dampened his fur and soon dampened his habit. Tuffy has learned that digging in is applauded only when efforts are sunk into the right places. And Randy found a tutor who inspired him and helped him establish good study habits. Now *both* Randy and Tuffy are digging in — Randy into his schoolwork and Tuffy at the scratching post.

126

Cat Nip:

A cat will be your friend but never your slave.
— *Theöphile Gautier*

Paws for Prayer:

Dear God, give me determination to begin, to continue, and to complete the duties before me. Amen.

"Whatever you do, work at it with all your heart, as working for the Lord."

Colossians 3:23-24

To get a grip on a job that's waiting, dig in with determination. Work past that imposing start, and get hooked on a dreaded task. Nothing productive in this world happens without hard work. Sharpen your character with a little gutsy determination, and sink your energies into that next project.

Cat Tip:

Cats scratch to loosen their claw sheaf, thereby making room for new growth. They also claw to leave their scent within their territories and to sharpen their claw tips for catching prey. Indoor environments need a provision for this natural scratching behavior.

The Tail End:

Nike's slogan "JUST DO IT"[8] is the simplest imperative for determination.

127

Make Your World a Playground

"When life gets intense, get out your toys and bat them around."

128

Katie

Katie kitten plays with delight and abandon. She chases her tail, bats at dappled sunshine on the wall, chases butterflies, peaks around corners, and runs in imaginary pursuits. She sidesteps and pounces, tosses her toys, and performs many brief acts of recreation for mere amusement.

At the age of twenty-six, it dawned on Bonnie that Katie had more toys than she. Katie had her catnip sock, her yarn ball, and her jingle bell ball. Did Bonnie have even three outlets for fun? The sad answer was no. *I have no crafts or a hobby for pleasure and relaxation. When people ask me what I do for fun, I answer honestly. "Nothing, really." My kitten understands play better than I do,* she thought.

Half embarrassed and half enlightened, Bonnie called me one day when she was weary from overwork. "Katie's world is a playground, but too often my world is a treadmill. Katie reminds me of my need to play," she said. Katie taught Bonnie something wonderful about life, and she set out to change. A couple of weeks later, I called her to see how she was doing.

"I know I'm a single career gal, but I'm now resisting my compulsion to work all the time. When I sense an obvious imbalance on the side of my work, I find a friend and share a fun activity. What a difference it makes. I don't wait too long before breaking from my routines. Now I actually schedule intermissions for the total purr-pose of fun."

Cat Nip:

A is for apple,
B is for boy.
C is for cat.
D is for dog, which follows <u>after</u> the cat, of course.

Paws for Prayer:

Dear God, help me to be as devoted in my play as I am at my work. Amen.

"There is a time for everything, and a season for every activity under heaven."

Ecclesiastes 3:1

If the practice of a sport, a hobby, or entertainment is absent from your life, break out of the sophisti-cat-ion of adulthood and play like a kitten. Try a little silliness and laugh at yourself. Meet your children upon their return from school adorned in a disheveled old wig. Go to an expensive restaurant and order appetizers and dessert. Go for a hike. Browse through a glitzy new department store, or hunt for bargains at a thrift store. Diversion and laughter can often refresh and restore better than sleep. When life becomes a dull habit, it is time to play!

Cat Tip:

Upper respiratory diseases (feline herpes virus, calici virus, FeLV, FIV and FIP) are a serious threat to kittens and are often fatal. Roughly 80 percent of those who recover remain carriers. The virus is spread when the kitten sneezes, and is also transmitted by direct contact from cat to cat via grooming and discharges from the eyes, nose, and saliva. Owners can disinfect their hands by using a mild solution of chlorine bleach.

The Tail End:

Without the rhythm of play, life is void of a necessary beat.

Everyone Benefits From Community

*"In community, joys are multiplied
and sorrows are divided."*

Old MacDonald's farm has nothing over our home since we adopted three orange tabby brothers. "Here a kitten, there a kitten, everywhere a kitten, kitten" is the appropriate tune around our house with Earl, Murray, and Myles at-large.

They best demonstrate their brotherhood by their community interaction. When one of the three wanders from sight of his siblings, a cry like a caterwaul alerts the others. Their oversized ears perk when the cry is heard and off they race to reunite with the straggler. Even in sleep, they are intertwined like a pretzel. The tangle of three overlapping kittens makes it difficult to determine which tail and head belongs to which rump and neck.

Upon waking, the trio then resumes their antics — Earl darting after Murray, Myles preparing to pounce, or all of them spinning about in a tail-chasing dervish. In spite of the 2,400 square feet to spread out upstairs and downstairs, they are seldom apart. They play, nap, and explore together. Community is their heartbeat.

133

Cat Nip:

The Andersons deducted the cost of their kittens, the cat food, the litter box, the toys, and other kitty paraphernalia from the most fitting among their budget cat-egories.
— Home Improvement!

🐾 Paws for Prayer:

Dear God, give me a mind-set that thinks communally and globally. Amen.

"All of you live in harmony with one another; be sympathetic, love as brothers."

1 Peter 3:8

Kittens remind us to be sensitive to the cries of those who are alone, separated from a group, or calling out for someone to enfold them. As we relate communally, expressions of mutuality, support, sharing, listening, giving, and caring make life better for everyone. When individuals function in community, no one is stranded or abandoned. Pleas for help are heard and answered. Offers of love supply aid while also uniting hearts. Make community a way of life.

🐾 Cat Tip:

Kittens require high-protein, high-calorie food two or three times a day. Don't overfeed. Fat kittens are not necessarily healthy kittens. Dry milk-formula kitten foods are popular with kittens. Make sure they are given fresh water daily and help reinforce litter box use by carrying them there after feeding, playing, or upon their waking.

The Tail End:

Brotherhood makes good sense, good religion, and good democracy.
— *Everett R. Clinchy*

Widen Your Horizons

*"Learn to look beyond
the end of your tail."*

Snowball

Snowball was a plump and tidy ball of snow-white fur who seldom ventured outdoors. Her world was no larger than the three-bedroom rancher she shared with the Emmetts. Snowball's horizons spanned little more than the view through the bay window, much less the broader expanse of the yard or beyond.

One day Mr. Emmett emptied Snowball's litter box and carried it to the backyard for a refill. It was a bright summer afternoon when back doors are left ajar. It had never been necessary to confine Snowball; she was content with her domain inside. But that day, she trailed a few cat tracks behind Mr. Emmett and followed him to the sand pile.

Unnoticed, Snowball watched as he loaded the box with fresh sand. When Mr. Emmett turned to empty the last shovelful, he was surprised to see Snowball, who had hopped into the litter box and was digging in. "Snowball," he exclaimed, "what are you doing in that box when you're surrounded by a truckload of sand!"

Mr. Emmett chuckled to himself as he pondered the irony. Oblivious to the mounds of possibilities in every direction, Snowball's horizons were limited to her habit of the box. Faced with the opportunity to expand and try something new, she was unmindful of her options.

Cat Nip:

Like those who ignore the fundamentals of grammar, cats make exceptions to most rules.

137

Paws for Prayer:

Dear God, my perspective is much too small for my needs, hopes and dreams. Help me look far and wide to You, the God of all things possible. Amen.

"(God)...is able to do immeasurably more than all we ask or imagine!"

Ephesians 3:20

As we ponder the scope of God's greatness, we realize how much we are like Snowball. Failure to look beyond ourselves narrows our vision and keeps us blinded to the possibilities on broader horizons. To see beyond the end of her tail, Snowball must look beyond herself. To believe beyond the limits of our capabilities, we must look beyond to God.

Cat Tip:

A cat who munches a mouse that has eaten a rodenticide (products designed to kill rats or mice) is at risk. Rodenticides interfere with the clotting properties of blood, causing internal bleeding. The strength of the product determines its potency. Signs of shock, weakness, rapid heart rate, shallow breathing, and cold extremities indicate the need for quick action by owners.

The Tail End:

Your horizons are as distant as your faith chooses to look.

Polite Confrontation Averts Angry Disputes

"Twitch your tail gently to express your annoyance lest you resort to scratching."

One summer the Newmans found a gray and white kitten at the park, whom they joyfully brought home with them. They named him Gus, and soon discovered that Gus wore his feelings in his tail. The action of his tiny tail matched the emotion of his loud mewing that day. His distress was plain. "I'm lost! Help me!" When the Newmans received no response to several posted signs, "Found: Gray striped male kitten," they offered Gus their home.

Gus continues to talk with his tail. When happily content, he lifts his tail and slowly and gently waves it back and forth. A contemptuous jerk of his tail indicates his distaste or disdain. When Gus spies the backyard squirrel, he belies his excitement by the quiver in the tip of his tail. Lashing his tail from side to side is a sure sign of anger or dominance.

The occasional visits of the Newman grandchildren are the only exposure Gus has had to children. Thus, he has little patience with them. Their sudden approaches, loud voices, surprise bumps, and clumsy attempts to hold Gus annoy him. A twitch of his tail is tell-tail evidence that his anger is building. Mrs. Newman warns the children, "Be careful, the kitty is lashing his tail. Leave him alone or he might scratch you." Her admonition usually stops them.

141

Cat Nip:

The game cats like best is "chase and keep."

Paws for Prayer:

Dear God, give me the courage to speak honestly and kindly to those I need to confront. Amen.

"Do not let the sun go down while you are still angry."

Ephesians 4:25

142

Timely displays of irritation usually avert explosions of anger. Even a cat does not resort to spitting or scratching until provoked beyond tolerance. The failure to confront someone about an irritation sets up both people for a later quarrel that may include exaggerations, accusations, and regrets — scratches are painful. If something is bothering you, speak up. Twitch your tail and give warning. A gentle confrontation is preferable to an angry outburst.

Cat Tip:

In the last four weeks of pregnancy, the female begins seeking an acceptable shelter in which to give birth. She may investigate cupboards and drawers and dig up soft padding like blankets or pillows, try out the arrangement, and then abandon it until she is satisfied with the right set-up. At this time, owners can provide the prepared delivery bed.

The Tail End:

Words spoken in anger are usually the best speeches you forever regret.

The Two-Way Toggle of Friendship

"When you're troubled, find the lap of a close friend."

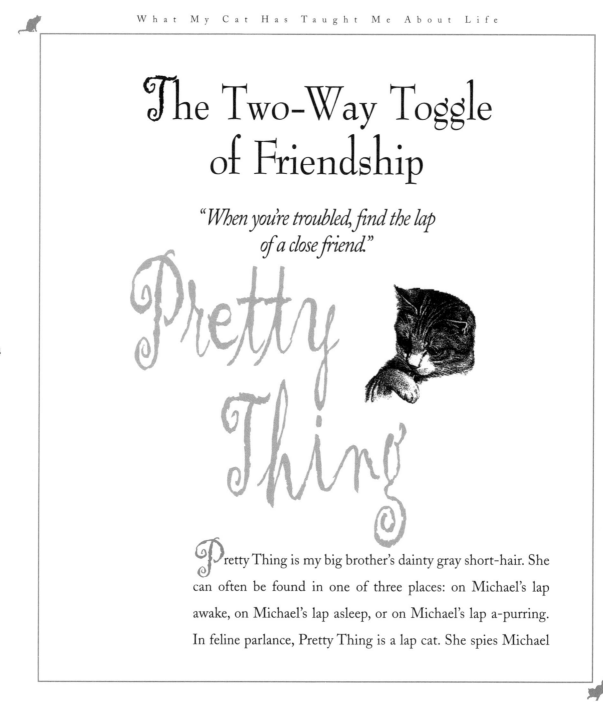

Pretty Thing is my big brother's dainty gray short-hair. She can often be found in one of three places: on Michael's lap awake, on Michael's lap asleep, or on Michael's lap a-purring. In feline parlance, Pretty Thing is a lap cat. She spies Michael in his rocker and cat-like she comes. One agile movement into the air, a slow methodical arranging of her body, a twist of the head for comfort, and she's settled into the lap of her closest friend.

Years of sharing life with a cat, means years of giving and taking. Michael is not abashed to admit their friendship is mutual. "She's been with me through a whole lot of life," he told me. "We have an understanding." When life deals its injustices, indignities, and insults, Michael finds solace in the comforting presence of Pretty Thing settled in his lap. Pretty Thing's obvious affection for Michael proves she is just as satisfied with his end of the friendship.

Some friends demand more from Michael and do not always give the returns that Pretty Thing does. Like all true friends, she is always ready to offer herself unconditionally. One of the greatest blessings of friendship is in the exchange of love and support.

145

Cat Nip:

Kitten, my kitten,
soft and dear,
I am so glad that we
are here
Sitting together just
us two,
You loving me and
me loving you.
— "My Kitten"
by Marchette Chute[9]

Paws for Prayer:

Dear Lord, thanks for being available through the kindness of my friends. Amen.

"A friend loves at all times."
Proverbs 17:17

146

Cats are not bashful about seeking warm laps. Then why be reluctant to seek out a warm friend? True friends specialize in caring. They are quick to offer and not hesitant to receive. When life roughs up the fur and scuffs the paws, solicit a little encouragement from a trusting friend. You will soon have the chance to reciprocate.

Cat Tip:

Annual recommended vaccines include FIP (feline infectious peritonitis), feline leukemia, and FVR (viral rhinotracheitis, calici, panleukopenia, and chalamydia). A rabies vaccine is recommended also under the timed direction of your veterinarian. These vaccines are essential for reducing the risks of contagious disease.

The Tail End:

True friendship is a plant of slow growth, and must undergo and withstand the shocks of adversity before it is entitled to the appellation.

— George Washington

Happiness Is an Outlook

"Don't believe those Fat Cats; possessions don't guarantee happiness."

Cable

Cable, an all-black short-hair, is a pampered pet. With a private bedroom in the home of his owner, a crystal food dish, a plush carpet scratching post, and a jeweled collar, Cable enjoys a posh life. He frolics in his outdoor enclosure with its runs, ramps, and ropes, carpeted cubbyholes, and look-out ledges. Felt mice toys dot the floor. Stray cats and middle-class neighbor cats regard Cable as the community "fat cat."

At the opposite end of the socio-economic scale is Buddy, a gray tabby. He contends that his lair is equally as comfy as Cable's. A discarded chenille bathrobe lines the orange crate that serves as Buddy's bed. His widowed owner stretches her pension to provide unfailing meals for him. His toys include birthday package ribbons, the widow's colorful yarn balls, and large grocery sacks left open for playtime. Cat-egorically, Buddy is not a "fat cat," but he feels like the happiest cat in all the cat cosmos.

149

The most deceiving myth of a materialistic society is the idea that you will be happy, only if you acquire certain things. Purchasing the latest and finest inventions might make life easier, but happiness is not a commodity born of invention or available by purchase. Happiness is a habit to cultivate, a praise to offer, a job to do, a song to compose, a bulb to grow, a child to educate, a compliment to give, and a chorus to hum.

Cat Nip:

Cats adore computers; there's often a mouse nearby.

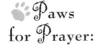

Paws for Prayer:

Dear God, help me value the enduring happiness of a positive perspective rather than the temporal happiness of perishable possessions. Amen.

"Happy is he who has... God... for his help, whose hope is in the Lord his God."

Psalm 146:5 NKJV

Happiness is not a possession to acquire but an outlook to adopt.

Cat Tip:

Providing a scratching post for your cat will spare the furniture. Rubbing catnip on the post is a good way to interest the cat in the post. If the cat resorts to textured wallpaper, furniture or draperies, speak a stern "No," and then escort the cat to the scratching post, hold the paws, and mimic a scratching motion on the post.

The Tail End:

God cannot give us happiness and peace apart from Himself.... There is no such thing.

— *C. S. Lewis*

Share the Sunshine

*"When you find a sunbeam,
share the warmth."*

Our neighbors across the street share both our last name and our love for cats. Among their four cherished cats are Callie and B.C. (shortened version of Black Cat). Each of the cats enjoys the morning sunshine, which beams through the large glass slider in their kitchen, glorifying the sheen of their colorful coats.

"When it comes to the matter of sharing the sunshine, however, Callie's disposition is not so sunny," says Sheila. "There's plenty of sunshine for everyone, but Callie is quite unwilling to share the light." Sheila showed me two classic snapshots of Callie pushing B.C. away from the sunbeam center. "The other cats spend many hours a day absorbing the rays together, but if Callie arrives at the window first, she tries to dominate the area. With her calico body pressed against the hot window, she firmly rebuffs others who come to bask with her."

Callie needs to learn that sharing the sunshine would add even more brightness at the window. Her owners have set a perfect example for her. Sheila and Forrest are models of unselfishness. Forrest works as a food service salesman and is frequently given samples of delicious food. Quite regularly the Andersons give their surplus to us. We become the beneficiaries of smoked turkey, seasoned-perfect pastrami, breaded poultry patties, energy bars, and other tasty fare.

152

Cat Nip:

This declaration was cross-stitched and framed in the home of cat owners: "This house under feline management."

Paws for Prayer:

Dear God, thank You for the warmth of the sun and Your radiant love. Amen.

"For the LORD God is a sun and shield."

Psalm 84:11

Hoarding anything usually lessens the blessing of ownership. Light bursts upon everyone when we move over and make room for others. I am grateful to a friend who was given two theater tickets and asked me to share the show. I was blessed when I offered my extra growth of perennials to a neighbor with some empty yard beds. Selfishness always diminishes the brightness of life. Like Callie, we all need to learn that unselfishness widens the block of sunshine beaming into our lives.

Cat Tip:

Two drops, no more, of citronella oil, (available through your pharmacist), put on a forbidden piece of furniture, will be repugnant to a cat and thus discourage his presence. Herbal and chemical sprays are also available for the same purpose.

The Tail End:

To love and be loved is to feel the sun from both sides.

— *Davis Viscott*

153

The Soft Sound of Humility

*"Walk softly lest you draw
attention to yourself."*

154

Stephanie is an apartment dweller who lives with her cat, Roman. She openly admits that she is the scaredy cat, not Roman, her hairless Sphynx. "I'm often startled by Roman's silent entrances. I always jump when I suddenly feel his chamois-like fur against my leg. When I'm engrossed in a book or working at my sewing machine, Roman startles me when he leaps into my lap."

The unannounced presence of cats is part of their delightful mystique. Their quiet movements give no hint of their approach. Felines walk on their toes with the soles of their feet seldom touching the ground. Only the soft click of a cat's claws on a hard floor betrays their presence.

Stephanie and Roman are well-matched. Stephanie also maintains a quiet demeanor. Though she has good reason to boast, she strives to be modest about her success as a skilled seamstress. In a drawer in her sewing room is a box filled with blue ribbons she has earned from dozens of contests, fairs, and competitions. When people admire her custom apparel she replies brightly but meekly, "Oh, thank you."

For cats, quietude is physiological. The pillow-like balls of their feet absorb the sound of each step. For people, a quiet appraisal of self is not as natural as the cat's gentle step. Though everyone wants to be humble, it is a rare characteristic.

155

Cat Nip:

Cats are confident, not conceited. Don't confuse their aplomb with arrogance.

Paws for Prayer:

Dear God, help me to respond with the proper balance between true humility and gracious acceptance of praise. Amen.

"Let another praise you, and not your own mouth; someone else, and not your own lips."
Proverbs 27:2

In the matter of personal achievements, it is difficult to be as quiet as a cat. Learn to sincerely appreciate the applause of others, but refrain from clapping for yourself. Learn from Roman to tread softly, especially when conversations center on your accomplishments.

Cat Tip:

Americans come in second to the Australians in their love of cats. Thirty-three percent of families down under own cats, followed by 30 percent in the United States.

The Tail End:

Humility is to make a right estimate of one's self.

— Charles Haddon Spurgeon

158

Individuality Is Your Imprint

"It's okay to be different from Garfield, Morris, and Sylvester."

Tucker, Carla's silver tabby, shuns the pillowed basket Carla gave him for Christmas. He prefers hard surfaces like the redwood picnic table and the backyard boulder. Tucker sleeps soundly on cement floors and formica shelves. He knows what he likes and makes no concessions by retiring on goose down comforters, soft laps, or barcaloungers. Tucker is in touch with who he is, and he does not deny his preferences — even when Carla mentions that "other cats" are connoisseurs of soft spots.

Carla admires Tucker's individuality. Tucker knows he is not "catty" like Garfield. He realizes he is much too shy to make television appearances like Morris, and he would not care to be black and white like Sylvester. Tucker is quite content to be himself.

Carla is just beginning to get comfortable with herself. "Unlike my neighbor who prefers gemstone jewelry and coordinated outfits, I'm a Levis and sweatshirts gal. Unlike my cousin who loves to travel to big cities, I prefer my rural farm community. I'm finally realizing it is okay to be who I am," Carla told me.

Differences make the world more colorful. "I see it all around me," Carla said. "My parents favor small gatherings and my in-laws throw extravagant parties. My grandparents chose the comfort of a small bungalow and my brother opted for a large two-story Tudor. We're all dif-fur-ent. Tucker would

159

🐾 Cat Nip:

Cats make their demands with such cunning that we respond to them as if they had made polite requests.

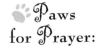

Paws for Prayer:

Dear God, I will remember today that "I gotta be who you made me to be." Amen.

"So God created man in his own image."

Genesis 1:26

probably add, 'That's why there are black cats, white cats, gray cats, and orange cats.'"

Being individualistic allows God to express the diversity of His image. Those who are brave enough to be themselves deserve commendation. Don't be a copycat. Glorify God's variety by being yourself.

Cat Tip:

Unspayed female cats, called "queens," are mature enough to reproduce between the ages of six to nine months. Schedule your kitten's alteration surgery between the ages of five to six months.

The Tail End:

When people <u>strive</u> to be original, they overlook the wonderful fact of their natural originality.

A Powerful Force Called Influence

*"Associate with those who are
a good influence."*

162

Barn Cat, abbreviated B.C., lived at the Folsom homestead for three years as the sole cat among four dogs, forty peacocks, one Shetland pony, and two horses. B.C. was content to control the mice population and make a single appearance each day to receive her bowl full of cat chow. Not only was B.C. aloof, she never meowed, purred, or vocalized otherwise. Not comfortable with people, B.C.'s best response was an infrequent rub of thanks at mealtime.

One day Amos, a neighbor cat, moved in. Amos was as loquacious as B.C. was taciturn. Every day, when the family went to tend the horses, Amos greeted them with his staccato yowls and his tag-along rubs. B.C. watched with disdain from a distance. Not inclined to converse with humans, B.C. simply observed Amos and his rambunctious communications with the family. Talking as he went, Amos was always underfoot. He once cat-apulted one of the workers, who landed chin-in-the-ground and eye-to-eye with Amos.

Months passed and Amos slowly influenced Barn Cat. The family began to hear B.C.'s soft purr at mealtime and noticed that she cautiously joined Amos in his greeting routine. She would even comment with an occasional meow. B.C. may never be sanguine, but she has come out of her shell. Amos is to thank.

163

Cat Nip:

Def-fur-nition of a Furanda: A porch where cats sit.
— *Jeanne Bjornsen*

Paws for Prayer:

Dear God, even as iron sharpens iron, let my influence sharpen those around me. Amen.

"Let your light shine before men, that they may see your good deeds."

Matthew 5:16

164

A good influence taught shy B.C. to interact in new and rewarding ways. The influence of example is a potent tool for affecting change. Whether or not conscious effort is made to influence others, example is constantly at work, wielding a positive or negative effect. Like Amos, be a good example; and like Barn Cat, be cautious about who influences you.

Cat Tip:

Remove a tick from your cat's body by pinching the tweezers as close to the cat's skin as possible. Twist counter-clockwise as you pull. This will better enable you to extract the tick's head and jaws. Apply a topical antibiotic to the area for two to three days afterward.

The Tail End:

The only thing more contagious than pink eye is a good example.

Let Your Limits Expand You

"Don't stick your nose in anything less narrow than your whiskers."

165

Fritzer squirmed. Fritzer yowled. Having struggled through a kicked-out hole leading under the sun porch, Craig's Maine Coon was afraid to attempt an exit. Fritzer suspected his portly body might get stuck. Craig surveyed Fritzer's situation with disgust. Before setting the cat free Craig admonished him, "A plump cat like you should pay attention to his whiskers!"

Fritzer's dilemma could have been avoided had he acknowledged his limits. One of the many incredible purposes of a cat's twenty-four whiskers is to measure width and thereby warn the cat not to enter an opening smaller than its girth. Fritzer is growing wiser. He hasn't wedged himself through the porch hole since the last incident. He is learning to value his whiskers and gauge his limits.

Craig also admits his limitations. He is a gardener but not a mathematician. He gladly lets Wendy, his math-wizard wife, manage the budget. It's a job she enjoys. Craig tends prize roses at the city park and earns many rosarian awards. He and Wendy have learned the lesson of accepting what they cannot do, thus freeing one another to excel at their true talents.

Before Craig and Wendy accepted their limits, they would often get squeezed into places where they didn't fit — just like Fritzer. By recognizing their abilities and accepting their limits,

Cat Nip:

The way to keep a cat is to place it outdoors, shoo it away with hand motions, and yell loudly, "Go away!"

Paws for Prayer:

Dear God, help me view my personal limitations not as restrictions but as opportunities to maximize my abilities. Amen.

"A man's gift makes room for him."
Proverbs 18:16

they have developed and expanded their strengths. Don't decry your inabilities; recognize your aptitudes and grow.

Cat Tip:

Because children sometimes use scissors indiscriminately, they should be taught the importance of a cat's whiskers and told implicitly never to cut them off.

The Tail End:

It is God the Creator who made limits, and the same God placed them within us for protection. We exceed them at our peril.

— *Dr. Richard A. Swenson* [10]

167

Moderation Pays Great Rewards

*"When looking over a goldfish bowl,
resist the temptation to binge."*

Morris

The first time I met Morris, I was astonished by his size. He sat with his front feet tucked under his chest and his round body sunk into the curvature of a large ottoman. I went home and described him to my family as "a basketball with four legs and a head." However, I am told that Morris' great proportions never hindered his leap to the bathroom counter to supervise Floyd's morning shave.

Morris weighed thirty-three pounds. His daily diet was not limited to the official recommendations — "one-half cup, twice daily." Morris' self-dispensing food dish encouraged his around-the-clock nibbling. His ample dimensions were not achieved by moderation! When my good friends the Damons took Morris for his vaccines, the veterinarian was alarmed by his weight. "Pat, you've got to get this cat on a diet." Though it was no laughing matter, he chuckled as he recorded the numbers from the scale. As they stroked Morris' rolls of fat, they discussed a lower calorie cat food and a limit to his feedings.

The next day Morris meowed for more each time his dish was removed. He paced around the vacant dish site and even sulked. His ever-present food supply was gone. Pat tried to assure Morris, "You're going to feel so much better, Morris, believe me." In a couple of weeks, the ounces began to fall off, then the pounds.

Cat Nip:

When a cat bolts from a corner, leaps over the couch, skids across the linoleum, rips down the hallway, scales the draperies, then drops to the floor and with a backward glance looks to see who's watching, it's time to give the creature some quality time.

169

Paws for Prayer:

Dear God, give me the strength to say "no" to excess and "yes" to moderation. Amen.

"Like a city whose walls are broken down is a man who lacks self-control."

Proverbs 25:28

One morning weeks later and ten pounds lighter, Morris leapt onto the bathroom counter with such agility, Floyd knew the diet was paying its benefits. That evening, the Damons watched Morris make an unprovoked run through the house. "Floyd, look at him! He feels the extra energy. Wait 'til we tell the vet."

Like humans, cat size varies with genes but is influenced by food intake. Moderation is a challenge for felines and human food fanciers alike. Defy the gratification of food in favor of a healthier body and a longer life. The results of intemperance are grave, but the rewards of moderation are great.

Cat Tip:

A paws-itive approach to leaving pets when owners leave home is to hire animal sitters listed in the Yellow Pages under Pet Services. Sitters visit the home to feed, water, and play with your cats (and/or dogs). Fees are sometimes comparable to boarding charges. Choose a sitter who is licensed, bonded, and insured.

The Tail End:

The truly hungry person will delight in parsnips, but the indulgent will binge on potato chips!

Value Is Not Based on Purr-chase Price

*"The best bargain in town
is a free kitten."*

172

During spring and summer, litters of kittens are born to breeders, private owners, and surprised residents who discover their yard shed has become a nursery for a mother alley cat and her litter. Signs scrawled on ripped cardboard and nailed to telephone poles post the seasonal offer — FREE KITTENS. The same two words are penned on boxes of kittens at yard sales. Free kittens are advertised in the newspaper and on bulletin boards in stores. How could anything so delightful be free?

When April Keller first viewed the wet kitten with the seeping eye offered by the neighbor girl at the front door, she was torn. Dolly, the family's costly Ragdoll, had passed away only weeks before and the hopeful little girl had heard. "Would you like this kitten, Mrs. Keller? He's free!" At that moment, April could think only of her husband's often quoted adage, "You get what you pay for." Kevin Keller believed that cost equated with value.

The kitten was soft gray with a white chin. His rain-sprinkled fur was begging for a dry towel and a warm rub. Just then Kevin stepped forward. One look toward the duet at the door and Kevin weakened his stand about pricey things. "Well, c'mon in, Lisa," he said. "Let's take a look at this little guy. He needs some medication for that weepy eye, huh." April went for a towel.

173

Cat Nip:

One fact that never remains hidden from cats is the sentiment a person holds toward them.

Paws for Prayer:

Dear God, spare me the error of devaluing what is free. Amen.

"Thanks be to God for his indescribable gift!"

2 Corinthians 9:15

"I guess we could let him sleep in Dolly's basket for the night," Kevin remarked. April could not help but think Dolly would be pleased with Kevin for offering the kitten her bed. As early as the next evening, the gray kitten had convinced Kevin that value is not based on purchase price. Silver, the free kitten, has happily remained with the Keller's since that damp night on the doorstep.

Cat lovers know better than anyone that the best things in life are free. Never forget that the most purr-ecious possessions you own may have cost you nothing and are perhaps the most valuable of all.

Cat Tip:

When purchasing a purebred kitten from a breeder, ask to see the parents to get an idea of the adult body conformation inherited by the kitten. Make sure the kitten has been wormed, request proof of vaccinations, and obtain a receipt for the sale. Acquire pedigree papers and request a plan for future care. The breeder is often the best contact for helping resolve later problems.

The Tail End:

I have learned that being denied what I cannot afford, and receiving freely what I can afford, are both blessings in disguise.

Always Make a Clean Impression

*"Don't spoil the chance to
make a good impression."*

Rufus

176

"Your name is Mud, you little mess maker!" scolded Sandra, as she watched Rufus track four muddy paws across her freshly mopped floor. Rufus had sauntered through the pet door at an untimely moment. His dusty feet met the damp floor and imprinted a trail of six-toed paw prints through the kitchen. His entrance hadn't left a good impression. Rufus made a quick and jaunty jump onto the rug beside Patches, his brother, as if to accuse, "It was Patches, not me!" But the six-toed paw print proved the truth of the matter.

The hubbub of Sandra's raised voice piqued Patches' interest, and he began to sniff the floor cleanser, still pungent in the air. Sandra saw it coming. "Oh, no!" Now Patches was headed for the floor. Gingerly he placed first one paw and then a second onto the all-intriguing surface. Sandra yelled, "Patches, get off there!" Her harsh words frightened him and across the kitchen floor he ran. A startled Rufus bolted behind him, leaving a third set of bad impressions on the doomed vinyl floor.

Sandra hunted down both cats and shut them inside the back room. "You two can keep yourselves occupied until my floor is dry." She returned to the kitchen and reached for the mop. Though she was annoyed, as she dipped the mop in the pail she told herself, *Thank goodness I can try again.*

177

Cat Nip:

Anyone who determines to have only one cat is plotted against staggering opposition: the cat population (not endangered), the cat appeal (irresistible), and the cat habit (deeply ingrained).

Paws for Prayer:

Dear God, give me pure motives behind all my attempts at making good impressions. Amen.

"If the LORD delights in a man's way, he makes his steps firm."

Psalm 37:23

178

Thankfully, Sandra could temporarily confine the cats and sponge up the cat tracks. Although correcting bad impressions in life is seldom that easy, consider this encouraging fact: You can always try again. Each person leaves an impression as unique as a thumb print, so strive to make your first impression your best one. But if it was a little muddy, try again — and watch where you step!

Cat Tip:

Some cats have as many as six and seven toes on each paw. Many of the cats owned by author and cat lover, Ernest Hemingway, were polydactyl.

The Tail End:

Always put your best foot forward, and make sure it is wearing a shoe that is shined.

Keep an Overhead Perspective

"Climb a tree. The view is better from on high."

Cats enjoy heights, much to the chagrin of cat owners like Sarah. The attaining of these heights includes landings on the top of her refrigerator, on the topmost shelf in her home office, and on the uppermost box in her storeroom. Outdoor cats are found on pinnacles of the roof, fence rails, and other high places like tall trees.

Sarah's black cat, Bianco, climbs trees to test the grip of his claws, to flee from dogs, and to humor the local fire brigade. Though he is inept at getting back down, like most perched cats, Bianco finds pleasure in the view from on high. The perspective above is different from the perspective below. Big things look smaller.

Bianco rallied the neighborhood and the fire department last summer when he refused to descend a tall pine. Shy Sarah was embarrassed by the arrival of the big red truck and the commotion of children gathered to watch.

The fireman quickly delivered Sarah's cat and placed him in her open arms. Hoping to console Sarah, the fireman said, "Yuh know, Ma'am, I think I know why your cat likes it up there. The view is great! From that top limb he can see that big ole barkin' dog over there is chained up. And I bet you didn't know you've got wildflowers growing behind that seven foot fence."

"No sir, I didn't." said Sarah. *Maybe Bianco's motive for climbing the pine was not just to agitate me,* she thought. If

181

Cat Nip:

Cats are not considered fuddy-duddies, or else the expressions "cool cat" and "hep cat" would never have been born.

Paws for Prayer:

Dear God, help me avoid tunnel vision. Remind me to survey my world with the broad perspective of a sky view. Amen.

"Set your mind on things above, not on things on the earth."

Colossians 3:2 NKJV

182

catching an overhead view of his world helped Bianco cope better on the ground, maybe she needed to do more climbing herself.

When Sarah's landscape becomes imposing, she now thinks of Bianco. If pressures, disappointments, and surprises depict a bleak scene on her horizon, she starts climbing. Prayer, uplifting literature, inspiring music, or counsel are means that help her rise from her ground-level perspective. Her outlook changes quickly when she views her circumstances from a higher plane. Solutions are more visible and problems appear smaller. The view is always better from On High.

Cat Tip:

Elderly cats need frequent brushing. As cats age they stiffen and find it more difficult to groom themselves in hard-to-reach places. Owners can assist.

The Tail End:

Perspective makes the difference
— *Some people grumble because
roses have thorns. I am thankful
that thorns have roses.*

— *Alphonse Karr*

Endnotes

[1] Unless otherwise indicated, all Scripture quotations are taken from the *Holy Bible, New International Version*®. NIV®. Copyright © 1973, 1978, 1984 by International Bible Society. Used by Permission from Zondervan Publishing House. All rights reserved. Scripture quotations marked NKJV are taken from *The New King James Version* of the Bible. Copyright © 1979, 1980, 1982 by Thomas Nelson, Inc., Publishers. Used by Permission. Scripture quotations marked NASB are taken from the *New American Standard Bible*. Copyright © The Lockman Foundation, 1960, 1962, 1963, 1968, 1971, 1972, 1973, 1975, 1977. Used by Permission. Scripture quotations marked KJV are taken from the *King James Version* of the Bible.

[2] Adapted from *Amazing But True Cat Tales,* by Bruce Nash & Allan Zullo (Kansas City: Andrews & McMeel, 1993).

[3] *The Cat Hall of Fame: Imaginary Portraits and Profiles of the World's Most Famous Felines*, by Terri Epstein and Judy Epstein Gage, illus. by Roger Roth (New York: Carol Publishing Group, 1994, 1996).

[4] Special thanks to the Carrs for permission to retell the story of Smokey and Buffalo.

[5] *The Cat Hall of Fame: Imaginary Portraits and Profiles of the World's Most Famous Felines*, by Terri Epstein and Judy Epstein Gage, illus. by Roger Roth (New York: Carol Publishing Group, 1994, 1996).

[6] Adapted from *Amazing But True Cat Tales,* by Bruce Nash & Allan Zullo (Kansas City: Andrews & McMeel, 1993).

[7] Adapted from *The Cats of Thistle Hill,* by Roger Caras (New York: Simon & Schuster, 1994).

[8] Slogan used with permission from NIKE, Inc.

[9] *Rhymes About Us,* by Marchette Chute (New York: E.P. Dutton, 1974).

[10] *Margin,* Used by Permission of NavPress, © 1992.

Bibliography

All About Cats, Tom Kuncl, Globe Digests, Globe Communications Corp., 5401 N.W. Broken Sound Blvd., Boca Raton, Florida 33487, © 1996.

Amazing But True Cat Tales, by Bruce Nash & Allan Zullo (Kansas City: Andrews & McMeel, 1993).

Cat Care, Dagmar Thies (Neptune City, NJ: T.F.H. Publications, 1989).

Cat Fancy, The Official CLA Club magazine, p. 48, May 1996, and p. 11, June 1996.

Cat Watching, Desmond Morris (New York: Crown Publishers Inc., 1986).

Cats in Color, Anna Pollard (London: Cathay Books Ltd., 1979).

Correct Quotes For Mac, (Novato, CA: WordStar International Inc., 1991).

Elbert Hubbard's Scrap Book, (New York: American Book-Stratford Press, Wm. H. Wise & Co., 1923).

Everyday Cat, by Mary Pyles (New York: Howell Book House, 1991).

Harper's Illustrated Handbook of Cats, by Robert W. Kirk, DVM, edited by Roger Caras (New York: Harper-Collins Publishers, Inc., 1993).

Name That Cat, by Doug Cassidy (New York: Crown Publishers Inc., 1992).

101 Questions Your Cat Would Ask Its Vet, by Bruce Fogle (New York: Carroll & Graf Publishers, Inc., 1993).

Persian Cats, by Ulrike Müller (Hauppauge, NY: Barron's Educational Series, Inc., 1990).

Thanks for Your Care, quotations from perpetual calendar. Used by Permission of Heartland Samplers, Inc. © 1993. All rights reserved.

The American Animal Hospital Association Encyclopedia of Cat Health and Care with Les Sussman (New York: Hearst Books, 1994).

The Arco Book of Cats, by Grace Pond (New York: Arco Publishing Co., Inc., 1969).

The Cat, by Muriel Beadle (New York: Simon and Schuster, 1977).

The Cat Hall of Fame: Imaginary Portraits and Profiles of the World's Most Famous Felines,
by Terri Epstein and Judy. Epstein Gage, illus. by Roger Roth (New York: Carol Publishing Group, 1994, 1996).

The Cat Lover's Dictionary, by Grace McHattie (New York: Carroll & Graf Publishers, Inc., 1994).

The Cats of Thistle Hill, by Roger A. Caras (New York: Simon & Schuster, 1994).

The 125 Most Asked Questions About Cats (And the Answers), by John Malone (New York: William Morrow and Co., Inc., 1992).

The Quintessential Cat, by Roberta Altman (New York: A Prentice Hall Macmillan Co., 1994).

The Silent Miaow, by Paul Gallico (New York: Crown Publishers Inc., 1964).

365 Cats Calendar, text by Lynn Strong (New York: Workman Publishing Co., Inc., 1995).

Understanding Your Cat, by Dr. Michael W. Fox (New York: Bantam Books, 1974).

$\mathcal{N}$iki and her three cats, $\mathcal{M}$urray, $\mathcal{M}$yles, and $\mathcal{E}$arl

About the Author

Niki says she grew up with a big brother, a dog, a cat, and God. Her mother implanted in her heart the wonder of a loving and all-powerful God so early in life that she does not remember ever being without a sense of His acquaintance. Her mother and father loved cats and agreed that home was not a home unless populated by at least one. Thus they had Crummy, Sam, and Walter, among a few.

Within months of Niki's marriage, she and Bob found an abandoned female kitten and named her Margo. Over the next years, there was Cynthia Ann, then Thomas, Gary, Thurlough, Dennis and Wes. And yes, two wonderful children arrived between the additions of the furry friends. Today the Andersons share their home with three tabby brothers, Earl, Murray, and Myles.

Niki enjoys many things besides her cats. She loves family, friends, new words, antiques, prayer retreats, teapots, and flowers. She and her husband of twenty-three years share a deep love for one another and a common love for cats. Their daughter Jodie is in college, majoring in journalism. Their son J.J. is in high school, majoring in studies on the weekdays and snow-boarding on the weekends.

Niki loves to create through composing. Her quotation on her author biography best expresses her motivation for everything she writes — "I delight in sharing the truths that have become vital in my own life."

Additional copies of this book
are available at your local bookstore.

Honor Books

The End